HEALER'S HERESY

Other books by

Alex Matthews

Secret's Shadow
Satan's Silence
Vendetta's Victim
Wanton's Web
Cat's Claw
Death's Domain
Wedding's Widow
Blood's Burden
Murder's Madness

HEALER'S HERESY

by

Alex Matthews

Alex Matthews

VEILED INTENT

PRESS

OAK PARK, ILLINOIS, USA

Library of Congress Control Number: 2010942189

ISBN 978-0-9794756-1-0

10 9 8 7 6 5 4 3 2 1

Dedication

For my husband Allen, who makes all things
possible.

Acknowledgements

Many thanks to all the people who helped in the
birthing of this book: my husband, Allen Matthews, who
brainstormed with me whenever I got stuck; my editor, Chris
Roerden, who would not accept less than my best; my fellow
writer, Nancy Carleton, who kept me honest; my publicist,
Barbara Young, who caught the mistakes I missed; former Oak
Park Deputy Chief Robert Scianna, who educated me on police
procedure; funeral parlor owner Lynne Williams, who
described what happens to bodies when they are removed from
the home; Burt Anderson, M.D., who provided medical
information; Judy Woll, a nurse who explained the workings of
a family practice clinic; Hallie Kolsen, who instructed me on
the ins and outs of Facebook; and Elizabeth Rose, who gave
me the title, Healer's Heresy.

Chapter 1

The back doorbell rang three times in rapid succession. Urgent. Imperative.

Startled, Cassidy McCabe sat up straighter on the waterbed and clicked off the TV. The numbers on the clock said ten-thirteen.

People almost never show up this late. Except for the neighbor who locked herself out. And twice when the police got you up at three in the morning to tell you your garage had been burgled.

From the den across the hall Zach Moran, clad in a heavy blue robe, headed downstairs. She was curious, but not curious enough to follow her husband in her current state of undress: a thin tee shirt, mid-thigh length, nothing underneath. *Besides, you and Zach have an unspoken agreement that he gets to play protective, chest-thumping male when you have late-night callers.*

She felt impatient for him to return and tell her who the door-ringer was. She told herself not to watch the minute number on the clock, which sometimes took incredibly long to change.

If it was the neighbor, Zach would come upstairs right away to get the key she had asked them to keep for her. *Or maybe not.* The neighbor was a cute thirty-something chick who buttonholed Zach whenever she could and engaged him in long flirty conversations. But Cassidy had nothing to worry about because Zach considered the neighbor a ditz. Or so he said. *Don't be ridiculous. You and*

Zach are so idiotically in love he's more likely to become a suicide bomber than an errant husband.

If it was the police, Zach would come up and tell her. Unless he forgot she was waiting to hear and went outside to inspect the garage with the cops. Her eyes slid toward the clock. Ten-sixteen.

So what makes you think you have to play passive wife? Just get dressed and go see for yourself.

She put on her panties, discarded the well-worn tee she slept in, then turned her bra inside out and twisted it around to the front to hook it. *Only a misogynist would design bras that fasten in the back.* She was zipping her jeans when she heard footsteps on the stairs and Zach came into the bedroom.

"It's a guy named Jordan Wenzlaff. Says he's a client. Insists he's gotta talk to you tonight."

"Jordan? Oh God!" Cassidy stared wide-eyed at Zach.

"I don't think you should go down. He smells like booze and looks pretty messed up. Plus there's a brown stain on his shirt that could be blood."

"I have to see him."

"No you don't. It's not in your contract that you have to see whacked out clients who show up after hours. Whatever jam he's got himself in can wait till morning."

"I'm going down." She grabbed a purple tee out of her drawer.

"He'll be gone by the time you get there." Zach started toward the doorway.

"You don't get to decide about my clients," she snapped.

"Then I'm coming with you."

"I'm going to take him into my office and close the door." She crammed her feet into her gym shoes.

"I'll wait in the kitchen where I can hear if you scream."

Cassidy went downstairs with Zach at her heels. As she hastened from the front entryway to her office behind the kitchen, she felt her heart thudding. She slowed down, taking a moment to compose herself, then went around the room divider at the rear of the kitchen. Jordan was pacing in front of the waiting room chairs.

He turned toward her. His usually stylish hair was in disarray and his eyes were red-rimmed and puffy. His face was drawn, cheeks flushed, forehead beaded with sweat. He reeked of alcohol just as Zach had said, and he'd zipped his jacket, hiding the stain on his shirt.

"I'm in trouble, Cass." He talked so fast his words ran together. "At least I think I am. Maybe they won't...no, they'll find out. I should've stayed away...I knew better than to go there. But it was the right thing to do. I couldn't just...." He swallowed and raked a hand through his hair. "I need a favor. A big one."

A shivery feeling ran through her. "I can't do anything for you unless you calm down and tell me what this is about. But first we need to go inside the office." *Where Zach won't be able to hear every word.*

She opened the door and waited for Jordan to proceed inside. As she crossed the threshold, her tension eased. Whenever she entered her office, her therapist part took over, a part that usually remained calm and confident even in the midst of crisis.

"Please sit down."

"I'm too jumpy. I can't sit still."

"We have some talking to do and we won't get very far unless you can sit down and focus."

Jordan stepped behind a low wicker table in the middle of the room and plunked his backside down on a pastel, fern-splashed sofa. Cassidy sat in her swivel chair across from him. One of his knees danced and he rubbed his right fist inside his left hand. At the moment he appeared to be every bit as much of a mess as Zach said. But in his normal state he was a stunningly handsome man, tall and limber, with finely sculpted features, thick chestnut hair, and a graceful way of carrying himself. When he'd appeared for his first session a couple of years ago, Cassidy had to force herself not to stare.

He was gulping air through his mouth.

Close to hyperventilating.

"Take a deep breath," Cassidy said in a slow, rhythmic voice. "Just keep breathing in...that's right...all the way down to your abdomen...now hold it...and let it out slowly." She repeated her instructions until his chest was rising and falling at a more normal rate.

"Now tell me what happened."

"She was"—his eyes welled up—"she was dead...when I found her." Tears started rolling down his cheeks.

"Who was dead?" *The woman who took out an order of protection against him?*

He silently shook his head. From the determined set of his mouth, Cassidy could tell he didn't intend to answer.

But he said she was dead already. That means he didn't do it. Or maybe he's wrong and she really isn't dead and you need to get her an ambulance.

Jordan covered his face with his hands and sobbed. Grabbing a handful of tissues, he wiped away the tears and mumbled, "I'm sorry.   It's just...I loved her so much."

"You said she was dead.   How could you be sure?"

"There was a bullet hole in her chest and her eyes were staring and she didn't have a pulse."

"Do you know how to take a pulse?"

"I worked as an EMT for a couple of years before college."

"How did you find her?"

His patrician face morphed from soft and vulnerable into stubborn.   "I'm not going to tell you."

Cassidy hesitated.   *Let it go.   It's not the most important thing.*

"So," she said, her tone low and soothing, "is this the woman you came to see me about?" *Please don't let it be her.*

"If I tell you who it is, you'll have to call the police."   His eyes filled again.   He lowered his head and raised a hand to his brow to shield them from her view.   "Sorry, Cass.   I wish I could say more.   I wish I could tell you all of it."   His voice cracked. "But you wouldn't believe me.   Nobody's going to believe me."

"You could try me."

He shook his head.   "The reason I'm here...." He pressed his palms together, fingers outspread. "I'm here to ask—no, to beg you—to destroy my records."

"What?"   She couldn't believe she'd heard him right.   "I can't do that."

"If the police subpoena my records, they'll be sure I did it.   But I didn't.   Those records could send me to prison."

Oh God!   Her skin felt tight.   Not even her therapist part knew what to do.

You're in over your head here.   There simply aren't any good options.

You don't want to hand over Jordan's records. According to the rules of confidentiality, not even the police have the right to see them.   But Jordan thinks they'll force you to turn them over.   So you could get in trouble for destroying them.

You need to talk to Zach.   This is too much to handle alone.   But you got in trouble once before for divulging confidential information.

She chewed on her lip.   *No good options.   But you have to do something.*

"I'll destroy your records if you give me permission to tell my husband what you said tonight and also what you said in sessions."   *Here's hoping Jordan doesn't know he's a reporter.*

Shock swept over Jordan's face.   "I thought everything was confidential."

"It is, unless you give me permission to tell someone else."

"But why would you want to?   What's he going to do?"

Find out if Jordan's old flame was just murdered.

"Lend moral support," Cassidy said, fabricating an excuse that sounded flimsy even to her.   "I'm taking a big risk here, destroying records the police will want to see."   *Except you know what's in them, so you can tell the police if you have to.*   "But I'm willing to do it if you give me permission to tell Zach.   And if you don't, I'll have to ask you to leave and the records will remain as is."

"How could you do this to me?   I trusted you."

Cassidy winced.   It felt all wrong to be treating a client this way.

"So what'll it be?" she asked.

"You'll destroy the records *and* not tell the police I was here tonight?"

"I'll destroy the records and I won't report your visit to the police."

"That's a promise?"

"Yes."

"Okay, you can tell your husband."

"I need you to sign a consent form." She pulled a form out of a metal file cabinet that stood in one corner of the room, filled in her part, and handed it to him.

He signed.

Chapter 2

As soon as the back door closed behind Jordan, Zach appeared in the waiting room. "You okay?"

"I feel terrible, but I don't have time to think about it now. You have to use LexisNexis to find the name of a dead woman."

"Whoa! I know you can't talk about clients, but did that guy just confess to a murder?"

"Actually, I can tell you everything. Jordan signed a consent form. But we need to find that name first."

"This guy with blood on his shirt gave you permission to spill the details of his private life to your reporter husband?"

"He didn't have a choice. He came here to ask me to destroy his records. I agreed to do it and not alert the police that he was here on condition that he let me tell you. He obviously doesn't know you're a reporter."

Zach's bronze-skinned face creased into a deep frown. "You're actually going to destroy his records?"

"It doesn't matter. I can always tell the police what's in them if I have to. Besides, I'm not legally required to keep records. Some therapists in private practice rely on their memory and don't even bother writing things down."

"Your word isn't nearly as good as documentation."

"It's too late. I already said I'd do it."

Zach leaned against the small counter next to her office that held a hot pot and the makings for tea. "Before we go any further, I want to know what you're getting us into."

"Back when Jordan was in therapy, he was obsessed with this woman doctor. She broke up with him, he started stalking her, and she took out an order of protection. After a while he seemed to come to terms with it and then he quit therapy. Tonight he told me he'd just found the body of the woman he loved." Cassidy folded her arms tightly against her chest. "He said he didn't kill her, but he must've done something because he's convinced the police will think he did. It seems likely the dead woman is the doctor, although it's been nearly a year since he terminated, so it's possible he's fallen in love with somebody new." *God, I hope it isn't the doctor.*

"We better get going. She might still be alive."

"Jordan was sure she was dead. He said she didn't have a pulse and he used to be an EMT."

"Yeah, but he'd had a few. Let's go see what we can find." Zach pushed off from the counter and headed toward the stairs.

Cassidy grabbed Jordan's folder out of her file cabinet and trotted after her husband. She found him in the room next to the den where he'd set up his computer equipment. He was seated in front of his monitor at one end of a long table. His printer and scanner were at the other end, with a clutter of office supplies in between. She sat in the chair next to his.

"You have anything on the doctor?"

"Just her first name." Cassidy flipped through the notes in Jordan's folder. "Claudia."

"We can get what we need from the order of protection. Spell Jordan's last name and give me some identifiers."

Cassidy spelled "Wenzlaff," then found a copy of a managed care form. She read off Jordan's date of birth and social security number.

"Now we're cooking." Zach entered the numbers and searched for the order of protection. "Here it is. The woman's full name is Claudia M. Leavitt." He recited a Hyde Park address. "Your client's prohibited from making any contact or coming within a hundred and fifty feet of her house or place of employment." Zach gave the print command.

"He used to drive by her house, ring her doorbell, call her at all hours of the day and night. He knew it was wrong but he had these urges he couldn't control. Along with his anger. He couldn't control that either."

Zach looked Cassidy in the eye. "I know you feel protective toward your clients, but you need to be objective. Regardless of what Jordan did or didn't do, the police and an ambulance need to get to the scene as soon as possible. We have to call nine-one-one and request a well-being check."

"No! The cops would trace the call and lean on me to tell them how I knew she was dead." Hearing a thump, Cassidy turned toward the opposite end of the table and saw their petite calico, Starshine, knock a pen and a pair of scissors to the floor. Cassidy turned back to listen to what Zach was saying.

"You have to tell them anyway. You've got important information relating to a crime."

She shook her head. "I promised Jordan I wouldn't tell the cops he was here."

"Look, Cass," Zach said in a tone he might use on an unreasonable child. "You were under pressure and you made a mistake. If Claudia Leavitt's been killed, the priority here is to catch the murderer, not keep a promise you shouldn't have made in the first place."

"Don't talk down to me! I couldn't tell the police about Jordan even if I wanted to because of confidentiality. And I don't want to. If the police knew Jordan asked me to destroy his records, it would make him look guilty, and I don't want to give them evidence they can use against him. Even if all I do is request a well-being check, the police will find the link between Jordan and me, and then they'll put the pieces together and figure out that he contacted me."

Starshine patted Cassidy's shoulder. Cassidy twisted around to pick her up, but she leapt to the floor and ran away.

"If you're determined to stay out of it—which I think is a big mistake—I'll make an anonymous call. Even though having a tipster in the mix could screw up the investigation."

"Wait. We're not even sure Claudia's the victim. The first thing we need to do is try to reach her by phone. If she answers, there won't be any reason to send the cops to her door."

Zach went into the bedroom with Cassidy at his heels, shuffled through the papers on his desk, and found his prepaid cell phone. He dialed, listened for a while, then disconnected. "I got voicemail."

"Hyde Park's only half an hour from here at this time of night. Let's go see if we can rouse her. If we can't, you can make your call."

"If we can, that means there's some other dead woman out there. In which case, I'm blowing the whistle on Jordan whether you like it or not."

Being high-handed. Taking over. Jordan's your client. Zach's got no right to interfere.

You're talking about a dead woman. Zach's doing what he should be doing and you're sticking your head in the sand.

Cassidy grabbed a jacket and waited on the stoop outside while Zach punched in the security code for the house. The April air, usually pleasant during the day, turned chilly at night. Dense shadows from the towering parkway trees spread across most of their yard. Grasping the stoop's wrought iron railing, she gazed toward Briar, the well-lit street that ran along the north side of their corner house. A heavyset black man walked a small fluffy dog on the opposite side of Briar. He was a familiar figure, a neighbor Cassidy exchanged pleasantries with. As usual, Oak Park gave off a sense of tranquility, but Cassidy's nerves were too jangly to take it in.

Zach joined her on the stoop and they headed toward the detached garage on the far corner of their property.

Chapter 3

As Zach steered his Subaru south on Austin Boulevard, the border between Oak Park and Chicago's gang-ridden west side, he said, "I still don't understand why you agreed to do everything this guy wanted. I know you needed leverage to get him to sign a consent form and you don't want to give the cops anything they can use against him, but it still doesn't make sense. You're the one who's always so hung up on doing the right thing." He looked over at her, his brows drawn together. "You have a crush on him or something?"

Her stomach knotted in anger. "That doesn't deserve an answer."

"You could tell me if you did. We'd work it out."

"No, of course not. I haven't looked at another man since we first started sleeping together."

"So why'd you do it?" Zach cruised down the entrance ramp and headed east on the Eisenhower. At this time of night, the six-lane expressway was nearly empty.

"The whole thing came at me so fast. I felt overwhelmed. I needed to talk to you, and I couldn't without getting his permission."

You're not telling him all of it.

Her mouth went dry. "I had a duty to warn and I didn't do it." She swallowed, moistened her lips, and continued. "During the time Jordan and Claudia were together, he acted out a lot. According to him, he never laid a hand on her, but he was possessive and controlling. He yelled, threw things, and punched a hole in her wall. Then, when she got the order of protection, he talked in therapy about wanting to kill her."

"And you *didn't* go to the police?"

"I did a thorough assessment and it seemed to me the threat was just a fantasy, not something he'd act on. I agonized over it. I was terrified he'd hurt her, but my gut said he wouldn't and my gut's usually right."

"Okay, but what does that have to do with the way you caved tonight?"

"It wasn't caving. He said he didn't do it and I believed him."

"You believed him? My God, Cass, how could you be so...naïve?"

"You were going to say stupid."

"But I caught myself."

Cassidy pressed her fist up under her chin and sat with Zach's question for a long time. "I believed him because I wanted to. Because if he did kill Claudia, I'd be partly to blame. I couldn't stand to think I'd been wrong."

A sports car came out of nowhere and sped past them.

"What you said about being partly to blame— you know that's not true. If some obsessive nut wants to kill his ex, he can do it, regardless of warnings or protective orders or anything. There's no way to stop these whack jobs. You should know that even better than I do."

"It feels like my fault."

"You just want to beat up on yourself."

"I knew you wouldn't understand."

Several minutes passed before either of them spoke again. Then Zach said, "Actually, I do understand. Remember that time I roughed up Bryce's mother?"

She did. Zach had told her that when he was in his early twenties, he was doing a lot of drugs and had an affair with a call girl who later gave birth to his son. She dumped him before he found out she was pregnant, and he reacted by inflicting a few bruises.

"I convinced myself she had it coming. I know how bad that sounds, but back then I was able to talk myself into believing it. It was the only way to avoid facing up to what a shit I'd been."

Hyde Park, the neighborhood surrounding the University of Chicago, was a racially diverse island in the midst of the almost solidly black south side. Populated largely by students and university personnel, it had a reputation for intellectual elitism.

They found the doctor's address on a block of single family homes. Zach stopped in the driving lane and they gazed at a two-story graystone residence, set back about thirty feet from the street, with a door in the center of the building, two wide windows flanking the door, and neatly trimmed shrubbery across the front. Light shone through closed blinds from both windows on the first floor and from two smaller windows upstairs.

Cassidy's scalp prickled. *She's not going to answer. You've been fooling yourself all along, clinging to the unlikely hope that the dead woman isn't Claudia.*

There were no legal parking places, so Zach pulled up in front of a fireplug. They climbed the steps to the front porch and Zach pressed the bell four times, allowing several seconds to pass between each ring.

"Let's go sit in the car and talk about the phone call I have to make."

"Maybe this bell doesn't work. We should try the back door before we give up."

"This is ridiculous."

"I know. But it can't hurt to do this one last thing."

"All right," he said, shaking his head. "Let me get my flashlight." He trotted back to the car, then returned and led the way around to the rear, where the only source of light was a yard lamp attached to the garage.

Probably just as well Zach's fucked up as often as he has. Makes him more tolerant of your own irrational impulses.

As Cassidy stepped onto the back stoop, she could feel something crunch underfoot. Zach aimed his flashlight at the canopy above. When she saw the broken bulb, her body went cold. He turned his light on the door. It stood ajar.

"Shit," he whispered. "Up until now, I was able to stay on the high ground, but I can feel myself slipping. With the door open, I wouldn't even have to break in, and we both know there's probably a body in there." He peered into her face. "You really ought to try and stop me."

"Moi? I'm the one who's been egging you on."

The furrows between his brows deepened. "Somehow I don't think it's a good thing that you've started acting more like me." He pushed the door open with the back of his hand and went inside. "Cops go nuts if they find out somebody's tromped through their crime scene. It contaminates the evidence."

Cassidy ran her tongue over her upper lip, then followed him into a dark kitchen, a square room with yards of counter space and a butcher block island in front of the sink. Picking up a familiar stench, she braced herself.

Zach said, "I don't suppose it would do any good to remind you that looking at corpses has never helped you sleep at night."

They headed toward a doorway that took them into a dining room. It was suffused with a soft light coming from the front of the house. The walls were covered with a contemporary paper in a feathery gold design. The streamlined table, credenza, and shelving unit were honey-colored oak.

The dining room opened onto a foyer, a brightly lit fixture overhead, a curving stairway at its far end. Cassidy gasped as she looked into the living room. They crossed the foyer's marble-tiled floor and stood under an arch to stare at the scene in front of them.

A tangled red bra tossed on the seat of an easy chair. A red thong draped over the shade of a lighted table lamp. A blue blouse crumpled on one arm of a loveseat. A pair of khaki pants heaped on the back of a sofa. Cassidy's gaze zeroed in on an amoeba-shaped brown stain about half a yard in diameter, near the center of the area rug. She surveyed the room, trying to ascertain where a body might be hidden.

Zach started walking around the perimeter.

"What are you doing?"

"Checking behind the sofa and loveseat. The body of a small woman might fit back there."

He squatted down to look behind the loveseat. "She's got a timer plugged in. Probably controls the lights."

He peered behind the sofa, then returned to the foyer. "They say that anybody who walks through a crime scene leaves something behind, but I doubt that any stray hairs from my head or dirt from the bottom of my shoes will influence the investigation."

Cassidy examined the staircase. "This is where she went." She blotted out the image of a wounded woman crawling up the stairs.

Chapter 4

Zach turned to look. Small splatters of blood were visible on three of the steps. He started upward. "Make sure you don't touch the banister."

"I know that." She spoke sharply, taking her edginess out on him.

As Cassidy rounded the curve in the staircase, she could see the short hall above. Light flowed from one of the open doorways. She tiptoed into the room, as if afraid to wake the sheet-covered body on the king-sized bed. Standing next to Zach, she looked down at Claudia.

The back of her head rested on a pillow. Her shiny dark blond hair was fanned out around her head, her eyes were closed, and the sheet was pulled up to her neck. Her skin was chalky and a small bloodstain showed on the sheet above the left side of her chest.

Zach wrapped a handkerchief around his hand and pulled the sheet back from Claudia's nude body. Cassidy could see a small hole on the doctor's left breast. Sliding his palm under her upper arm, he said, "She's not quite cold. It's only been a few hours."

"The killer shot her downstairs, undressed her, then arranged her body like this."

Zach drew the sheet back up. "I didn't see any blood on her clothes so he probably made her strip first. This has all the earmarks of a woman killed by her lover. Or her ex."

"Jordan said she was already dead when he found her."

"He *found* her? You mean, he just happened to be wandering through her house? Given that she took out an order of protection against him, what possible reason could he have for being here?   I think he got himself a gun, tanked up on booze, and broke in with the express purpose of killing her."

Cassidy scowled at her husband.   "Sarcasm is such a great way of getting your point across."

"Oh, and that wasn't?"

She gritted her teeth.   *What made you think you needed his help anyway?   You should have handled this on your own.   Except you don't know how to use LexisNexis.*

Taking a deep breath, she forced herself to concentrate on the murder.   "Any idea why there's so little blood?"

"The bullet must've gone directly into her heart. If the heart stops instantly and it isn't a through and through, the victim doesn't bleed much.   I'd guess a small caliber bullet at close range."

Cassidy started to shiver.   "I've seen enough."

"Yeah, we should get out of here."

Cassidy fastened her seatbelt, then looked over at her husband, who'd made no move to fasten his. He'd turned sideways to face her, his arm resting on the steering wheel.

"I know I said I'd make an anonymous call but I didn't think it through."

"You're trying to back out."

"Cass, listen to me.   We're talking obstruction here.   If I report the murder anonymously, they'll tape Jordan's voice and compare it to mine.   Then they'll have proof that some unknown male had prior knowledge of the crime.   Even if Jordan confesses, the defense could use my anonymous call to raise reasonable doubt."

"But if you give them your name, they'll force you to explain how you knew about the body, and then they'll use electric prods to make me tell them about Jordan's visit.   Once the cops discover he wanted his records destroyed, they'll really go after him.   In fact, they might come after me too, for agreeing to do it."

"They don't use electric prods anymore."

"A subpoena then."

"So you're willing to take the chance that my call will result in a murderer getting off?"

"I'd rather see a murderer go free than an innocent man spend the rest of his life in prison. Besides, I promised Jordan I wouldn't tell.   I can't stand the idea of being presented with a subpoena and forced to give out confidential information."

"Well, I know how you feel about keeping your promise.   If I promised anonymity to a source, it'd take electric prods to get it out of me."

Zach took out his prepaid cell.

"Give it to me," Cassidy said.   "I'll do it."

Ignoring her, he punched in 9-1-1.   "I was on the sidewalk in front of 5720 S. Kenwood Avenue and I heard a woman screaming."   He ended the call.

"That shouldn't affect the investigation."

"I doubt they'll believe me.   The house is set quite a ways back from the street and the windows are closed.   And if I'd really heard screaming, why would I wait so long to report it?"

Zach dropped Cassidy off by their gate, then drove on to the garage.   The night's events weighing heavily on her, she trudged toward the back door. She lifted her eyes to the stoop, hoping Starshine would be waiting for her.   Instead, the overhead bulb spotlighted an orange cat at least three times the size of their calico.

Cassidy, who'd had considerable dealings with strays, hoped it wasn't a homeless cat looking for a handout. *Because if it is, your sappiness quotient won't let you turn it away.* In her experience, few strays had allowed her to get close enough to touch them, so she expected the orange cat to run. But it stayed on the stoop, closely eyeing her approach.

Maybe it isn't a stray. Maybe it's a family cat that's lost. Or been dumped by its owner. Her back teeth clenched. Few things made her angrier than people who discarded their pets.

She remembered coming home a few years earlier and finding a barely-out-of-kittenhood Starshine on her stoop. The calico hadn't run either. She'd slipped inside when Cassidy opened the door and claimed Cassidy's house as her own. *Well, you can't let that happen again. Starshine's determined to be an only cat, and she'll make your life miserable if you force her to share. But if the orange cat's in need of a home, you'll have to take it in and try to place it in a shelter.*

When Cassidy was three feet from the bottom of the steps, the cat arched its back, puffed up, and hissed. She stopped abruptly. She'd never encountered a cat aggressive enough to try to face down a human.

"Shoo! Go away!" She waved her arms to scare it.

Moving slowly, the cat started down the steps toward her. She couldn't believe it. The cat was acting as if it might attack.

"Get your ass out of here now!" Zach bellowed from behind her. She turned to see him fast walking toward the cat.

The creature stood its ground for a moment, then slid off the other side of the steps. Cassidy ran around the stoop, hoping the cat had disappeared, but it stood facing her near the corner of the house. Zach yelled at it again, and it turned and slunk toward the street. The view Cassidy caught of its rear end confirmed her opinion that it was a tom. It had balls the size of grapefruit.

"That cat's testosterone level has to be off the charts," Zach said.

"What I want to know is where Starshine is." Cassidy dashed up the steps and unlocked the door. "If she came out while that monster was here, he could've taken her apart." The calico had a cat door in a basement window, which allowed her to come and go as she pleased.

Zach looked down at the concrete surface of the stoop. "I don't see any blood or fur so she's probably all right."

Chapter 5

Cassidy went inside and called, "kitty, kitty." Within seconds, Starshine strolled into the kitchen, sprang onto the counter, and sat next to her bowl.

"I'm so glad you're safe." Cassidy scratched the side of the cat's face.

Starshine uttered an amiable *mwat.*

"What are you saying? That you're happy we're home? That you want a midnight snack?"

Don't kid yourself. It's always food.

Cassidy hesitated. She'd been restricting the once blimped-out cat to two meals a day, plus the one Zach snuck in behind her back.

Yes, but this has been such a terrible night you can't deprive yourself of the pleasure you get from making your cat happy. She opened a can and plopped a large spoonful of food into Starshine's bowl.

"We have to keep her in tonight," she said to Zach.

He headed down the basement stairs, locked the cat door, then returned to the kitchen. "You know that knob we turn to close the flap? It's getting creaky. We may have to put in a new cat door before too much longer."

"I don't want to think about it tonight."

Zach went into the dining room and fetched a bottle of brandy and two snifters. "I need a drink. And so do you."

She used to bristle when he prescribed alcohol for her after a grueling experience, but she'd never quite been able to refuse the glass he put in her hand. Over time, she'd come to realize he was usually right in his assessment of her mental state. He pushed booze only when he could see that her anxiety level had climbed so high she needed chemical assistance to bring it down.

She initially considered it a weakness to take the glass he pressed on her. She thought that if she were a stronger person she'd tough it out, or do yoga, or meditate instead of tranquilizing herself with liquor. But now, drinking a snifter of brandy when she felt like cracked glass on the verge of shattering seemed no worse than taking an aspirin to relieve a headache. Just as long as she didn't need it too much or too often.

Zach poured two fingers, tossed it down, then splashed a generous amount into both glasses.

They were in the waterbed, Zach with his knees bent and his back against the headboard, Cassidy at a right angle with her back against his knees. Starshine, purring rambunctiously, lay stretched out next to Cassidy. Zach rubbed Cassidy's neck while Ray Charles's gritty voice crooned *Georgia.*

Cassidy sipped her brandy, her cracked-glass feeling gradually subsiding. "I never should have made that promise to Jordan. It was unprofessional and it kept me from doing what I should have done, which is to request a well-being check like you said."

"It's over and done with. No point looking back."

She twisted around to glare at him. "I know you don't like it when I go into my angst mode, but I need to talk about it." She scratched the top of Starshine's head. "The problem is, I've become so damned dependent. When I was married to Kevin, I thought I could do anything. Anything, that is, except keep him out of other women's beds. But now, whenever I get in a sticky situation, I feel like I have to go running to you for help."

"What's wrong with that?"

"Women need to be independent. They have to be able to take care of themselves."

Zach shifted around so he could sit straighter, then began massaging her neck again. "As you well know, I used to be determined not to need anybody. I learned early in life that when you need people, they have power over you, they can hurt you. And that's certainly been the case with you. You back me into corners and force me to do things I don't want to do. You convince me to make anonymous calls I shouldn't make. You get yourself beaten up and it nearly kills me. But there's no question that it's worth it.   We're both better off needing each other than going it alone."

"But you never lean on me the way I do on you."

"You're just trying to get me to talk about feelings, which I've already done more of than I intended to. You know I'm every bit as dependent on you as you are on me, only in a different way. Now if you don't shut up, I'm going to get myself another brandy and then you'll be pissed at me for drinking too much."

Cassidy, who usually had difficulty crawling out of bed at eight A.M., found herself awake at five-thirty, unable to stop an endless loop of scenes from the previous night that played in her head. She slipped out of bed, careful not to disturb Zach. Starshine, who spent her nights curled up between their heads, bounced down and pranced at her feet. Cassidy put on her nightshirt and slippers and went downstairs.

The calico ran ahead, jumped onto the kitchen counter, and chirped gleefully. She loved mornings as much as Cassidy hated them.

"It's too early for breakfast. If I feed you now, you'll be off schedule all day and then you'll expect an extra meal tonight."

Starshine's moist green eyes fixed adoringly on her human's face.

Cassidy knew she was being manipulated. She recognized that the cat traded love for food, and when she didn't get her way could turn hostile in the blink of an eye. But she still couldn't resist what appeared to be an outpouring of affection from a creature who frequently couldn't be bothered to acknowledge her existence.

She fed the calico and put on a pot of coffee. Starshine polished her bowl, then washed her face, ears, and other parts of her anatomy. When she finished her ablutions, she trotted to the back door and began to howl. Even though she had her own private entrance—now locked, although she didn't know it--she preferred to be waited on.

Cassidy started toward the door, then remembered the enormous orange tom waiting on their stoop the night before. *Waiting for what? For Starshine to come out so he could eviscerate her?* A chill crawled up Cassidy's spine. She wished she could keep her little princess in the house indefinitely, but her previous attempts to corral Starshine had never worked. The cat either punished Cassidy by sulking in the basement or waited by the back door and dashed out when someone opened it. She usually zipped past unwary clients, but she'd been known to get past Cassidy and Zach as well.

"I may not be able to keep you in as long as I'd like, but I can keep you in until you out-finagle me." Cassidy deposited Starshine on the other side of the basement door so she couldn't pull her streaking-outside-when-the-back-door-opened trick.

She filled her purple cat mug, grabbed a bag of peanut butter cups, and went up to the computer room to get Jordan's file from the table where she and Zach had been sitting the night before. Although she knew there probably were advantages to computerizing her records, she hadn't been able to motivate herself to go digital. Handwriting her notes on yellow legal pads still seemed easier, even though she used the computer for a variety of other tasks. *The thing is, you have this basic resistance to technology, which doesn't make sense but you can't get rid of it.*

She carried the file into the den where a row of windows extended across the two exterior walls. She could see a glimmer of light above the rooftops to the east. Sinking into her leather chair, she propped her slippers on a footstool and opened the file. Zach's chair stood next to hers, with an entertainment center facing the chairs. This was one of her favorite places for sitting, both because of the natural light that flooded the room during the day and the way the small chair fit her diminutive frame.

She nibbled on a Reese's while she read through the notes she'd written about Jordan's therapy sessions. In his first session, dated almost two years earlier, he'd told her he recently met a woman doctor and it had been an instant take on both sides. But his jealousy and rage had driven away all the women he'd loved before, and he was afraid the same thing would happen again unless he got help.

Cassidy had had her own struggle with jealousy during the early stages of her relationship with Zach, but her problem stemmed from having spent too many years with a philandering first husband. Once she learned that Zach wasn't going to lie or cheat, her jealousy disappeared. Jordan's jealousy was much more deep-seated. He felt intrinsically unlovable and therefore expected that once any woman got to know him, she'd leave.

Cassidy reached for another peanut butter cup from the bag sitting on a side table next to her chair. She finished reading one sheet of paper and went on to the next.

During the first stage of Jordan's relationship with Claudia, he put her on a pedestal and courted her lavishly. During the second stage, he grumbled over minor complaints: she was a workaholic; she didn't make enough time for him; she had dinner with her girlfriends on a night they could have been together.

During the third stage, he acted out violently. The first episode occurred when she started telling him about one of her previous boyfriends. Jordan admitted in his next session that he'd called her names, threw the flowers he'd brought into the trash, and broke one of her chairs. Cassidy struggled to get him to see that Claudia had done nothing wrong, but she was unable to break through his insistence that she should have known better than to talk about other men.

In succeeding sessions Jordan reported a string of angry outbursts. Through his work in therapy, he came to understand that his behavior was unacceptable, but understanding did not translate into the ability to control his temper. A day came when Claudia told him she'd made plans to meet an old boyfriend for lunch. Jordan followed her to the restaurant and sat at a table next to hers. When he returned to his condo, there was a message on his voicemail from Claudia saying she never wanted to see him again. Jordan proceeded to harass her, and a few weeks later she took out an order of protection.

Chapter 6

Closing the folder, Cassidy drained her mug. She recalled that her first session with Jordan after Claudia took out the order was the most difficult of her career. She'd written a lengthy set of notes to document it, but not eager to relive the experience she decided to take a break before continuing.

The high decibel squabbling of birds that had built a nest under her window air conditioner drew her attention. She assumed they were only a mom and dad but they sounded like a large dysfunctional family. Crossing the room to stand in front of the south-facing windows, she looked at a row of backyards stretching halfway down the block. Three small children, already outside, were climbing into their huge redwood playhouse.

She returned to her chair and picked up her notes. Two days before the critical session, Jordan had called to tell her about the order of protection. He sounded so distraught over the phone, she knew she was in for a grueling hour.

When she walked into the waiting room that day, she came to a halt at the sight of him. His jaw was clenched, his handsome face carved into angry lines. They took their usual places in her office, Cassidy in her swivel chair, Jordan on the sofa.

She folded her hands in her lap. "You look pretty upset."

"Well, wouldn't you be?" He scowled at Cassidy. "That woman played me. She knew how hard I was working in therapy—the changes I'd made. She said she could see I was trying and she'd give me time. And then she...Someone better comes along and she dumps me."

Cassidy sighed inwardly. *Just started taking responsibility. Now he's back to blaming her.*

'Course he is. Spent the whole hour sobbing after she broke up with him. How could he not be regressing?

Jordan clamped his hands over his knees, squeezing so tightly his knuckles turned white. "She's going to pay."

Cassidy felt a spurt of alarm. "Pay how?"

"I keep imagining myself standing in front of her with an automatic. She's begging for her life just like I begged for a second chance."

Cassidy's stomach churned, but she kept her body loose and her expression sympathetic.

Deep ridges appeared on Jordan's brow. "She's begging but I don't listen to her any more than she listened to me. Then I pump her full of bullets and she goes down. She takes a long time to die. She can't talk but her eyes are still begging. And I stand over her and watch her bleed out."

Cassidy asked in a matter-of-fact tone. "Do you see yourself doing it? Or are you inside your own skin, looking through your own eyes?"

"I'm fuckin' doing it, man. I don't see myself— just the gun in my hand and Claudia begging for her life."

This is bad. Not just a fantasy. Actually rehearsing it.

"Do you have a gun?"

He shook his head.

"Have you ever had one?"

"No, but I hear it's easy to get one on the street."

"How would you go about doing it?"

His features displayed a look of mild confusion. He rubbed his left forearm with his right hand. "I haven't thought about it."

Cassidy swiveled her chair slightly, her eyes never leaving his face. "Do you ever think of killing her some other way?"

"It's always the same. I see her falling backward, bleeding from all the holes I put in her."

"Do you feel an urge to do it?"

"I think about it a lot. But I haven't felt like trying to get a gun or anything."

The tension in Cassidy's chest eased slightly. "Is there anything that would stop you from doing it?"

"Well, I know I'd...." He swallowed. "I'd never get away with it. What with the order of protection and all, there's no way I wouldn't end up frying for it."

She felt almost dizzy with relief. Swiveling her chair again, she tried to think if there were any other questions she needed to ask. She remembered that most of his outbursts had occurred after he'd downed a couple of scotches. She'd tried to get him into A.A., but he'd insisted he didn't have a problem.

"How much are you drinking?"

"Just a glass of wine now and then. I'd like to cut loose and get loaded but I'm afraid of what I might do if I let myself drink."

Cassidy locked eyes with him. "You realize you'd lose everything if you acted out this fantasy?"

He nodded.

"Will you promise to call me if you feel the least urge to harm her? Or if you start planning ways to get a gun?"

He looked out the window for several beats, then faced Cassidy again. "I don't want to make my life any more of a mess than it is already. I promise I'll call."

People usually ignore promises but it never hurts to have one.

Chapter 7

After that session, Cassidy had spent the next couple of days in turmoil. If she believed Jordan posed a danger to Claudia, it was her duty to tell the police. But it took Cassidy a while to make up her mind what she believed. One part of her said she shouldn't take chances. That Jordan could get drunk and act out at any time. Another part said that since he wasn't feeling an urge to do it, didn't have a plan for getting a gun, and understood the consequences, the odds of his hurting Claudia were low. This part also argued that he needed to stay in therapy, and if Cassidy reported him, she'd never see him again. Her intuition, which had served her well in the past, convinced her that Claudia was not at risk. So Cassidy had done nothing.

She picked up a pen and tapped the clicker against her teeth. *Now Claudia's dead and Jordan's the most likely suspect. Does that mean you screwed up?*

Cassidy understood that even if she'd gone to the police almost a year earlier, she couldn't have prevented the murder. *But if Jordan did kill her, you made a bad call. There are times you get too empathic. You care so much about your clients you think they're better than they are.*

Jordan had continued in therapy for three more months, and by the time he finished, he seemed to understand that he was responsible for pushing Claudia away. In his final session, he told Cassidy that the next time he fell in love, he would call her before he did anything else.

At seven-fifteen, with a thin light showing through the window above her sink, Cassidy made fresh coffee. Plaintive wails came from the other side of the basement door but she ignored them. She refilled her mug, poured a second mug for Zach, and returned upstairs. She could hear him snoring lightly as she went around to his side of the bed.

She placed his mug on his nightstand and pushed a button on the clock so the alarm wouldn't go off. He was sleeping on his side, his face toward her, his toes sticking out at the end of the bed.

She kissed his stubbly cheek.

He took one more deep breath and opened his eyes. "This is backward. I'm supposed to bring you coffee."

"I couldn't sleep so I got up and read Jordan's file. Why don't you come in the den and we can drink our coffee together."

He donned his plush blue robe, carried his mug across the hall, and sat in the leather chair next to hers. After taking a gulp of coffee, he asked, "So, what else can you tell me about the guy who showed up at our door last night?"

"I already mentioned that he had the typical characteristics of an abuser—angry, possessive, controlling—but few people other than the women he fell in love with ever saw that side of him. On the surface he seemed like a prize. A creative writing teacher at Columbia College and a successful poet. He's been published in several magazines and performs regularly at poetry slams. Claudia heard him at the Green Mill and was so taken with his work she stayed to talk to him afterward."

Zach's robe slipped off one knee and he pulled it up. "Yep, I've written plenty of stories about guys like that."

Cassidy's fingers tightened on her mug. "You mean guys who kill the women in their lives?"

Zach shook his head. "That's not what I meant to say. I'm not quite awake yet."

"But you've made it clear that's what you think."

"I did last night. But now that I've had a chance to sleep on it, I realize I need to keep an open mind. I've seen so many situations where things aren't what they appear to be, I've learned it's a mistake to jump to conclusions. My initial response is to go with the obvious, but then I try to step back and look at other possibilities."

"I usually don't have much sympathy for abusers—men or women—but I liked Jordan." She pulled the footstool closer so she could bend her knees and rest her toes on its edge. "After several months in therapy Jordan was able to acknowledge that his acting out was wrong, and he even reached a point where he felt genuine remorse, something most of these types never do. And he was so vulnerable. I can't tell you how many times he cried in sessions. Then afterward he couldn't apologize enough."

"So, are you still convinced he's innocent?"

Cassidy noticed a tuft of black hair sticking up on the back of Zach's head. "I think he *may* be innocent. In his fantasy he shot her full of bullets and watched her die. That's pretty different from shooting her once, then carrying her upstairs, laying her on her bed, and pulling a sheet over her."

"You do realize I'll probably be covering the murder, don't you?"

Cassidy blinked. "I hadn't given it any thought." As the idea sank in, she felt a flicker of anticipation. "Does that mean you'll be investigating it?"

"I doubt it. Claudia Leavitt isn't a celebrity. And if the police charge Jordan, the case will be officially closed."

"But if you really wanted to investigate, your editor would let you, wouldn't she?"

"Are you forgetting she's only been my editor for a few months? Libby doesn't know me like John did. She's gotta prove she's in charge and I've gotta prove I know what I'm doing."

Zach had worked for John Hammersmith for more than a dozen years. During that time, Hammersmith had developed enough confidence in Zach to let him set his own agenda. But after the editor retired, Zach's freedom had been significantly curtailed.

Cassidy said, "I bet you could get Libby to let you investigate. You can talk people into almost anything."

"Except you. With you it's the other way around." His eyes narrowed. "Why are you pushing on this? Because you want in on it?"

"I need to know the truth. I won't be able to put this to rest until I do. It's certainly possible the police will arrest Jordan, but that doesn't necessarily mean he did it. We both know that a lot of innocent people have been convicted."

"Are you still blaming yourself? Your failure to warn Claudia over a year ago has nothing to do with her death."

"This isn't about blaming myself. It's more about...."

"What?"

She focused on the voices in her head. *You might've made a huge mistake. Might've been completely wrong.*

"About my judgment...and intuition. About whether I knew Jordan as well as I thought I did."

"Okay, I get it. But even if I could get around Libby on this, I wouldn't want you working with me."

"Why not? We've worked on your investigations together before."

"First, there's no good way to explain why I'm bringing my wife with me on interviews. Plus, it's likely Libby would find out, and she'd think I was nuts. Or if not nuts, completely unprofessional."

Cassidy reached over and patted his knee. "Come on, Zach. You've got a special talent for making things up. You can explain away the most outrageous things and people always buy it."

Zach clamped his lips together, one corner of his mouth pulling down.

"Wait, you said 'first.' That must mean there's a second."

"I have to be objective. I can't start an investigation with any kind of bias. You, on the other hand, want to prove Jordan innocent. Which would mean we'd end up fighting. I don't want to set myself up for that."

"No, you're wrong. I'm not out to prove anything. It's what I said before—I just need to know the truth. I need to find out if my intuition was completely off base, or if I can still trust it."

Zach's blue-gray eyes turned steely. He searched her face, apparently trying to determine how much trouble she was likely to cause him. Then he softened.

"Oh hell. Once you decide you're going to do something, I've never been able to stop you. Okay, I'll see if I can convince Libby to let me dig into Claudia's murder. If she says yes, we'll make it a joint venture."

"Can you call her now? Or is it too early?"

"I can get her on her cell. I'll tell her a police source contacted me last night and described the crime scene. Then I'll say I'm putting the murder at the top of my list. I may have to do some arm twisting because this kind of story usually isn't worth more than a few inches inside Metro."

Chapter 8

Cassidy stood, holding Jordan's file against her chest. "While you're calling, I've got some paper to dispose of." She went into the computer room and turned on the shredder. It made a loud growling noise as it chewed up her notes.

A few minutes later Zach came in and sat in front of his monitor, rolling his chair off to the side so he could see Cassidy, sitting on the other side of the computer table.

"Libby didn't make it easy. She had some other stories in mind for me today and wanted me to just write up the facts of the murder. But I kept insisting there had to be a sexy story behind a crime scene like that, so she finally agreed to hand off my assignments to other reporters and let me spend a couple of days on the Leavitt murder."

Moving his chair back in front of the screen, Zach began typing and clicking his mouse.

"Who do we talk to first?"

"Next of kin. I'm finding out who that is now." Zach tapped keys and clicked some more. "I've got it. Claudia is survived by her mother, Ellen Leavitt, and her sister, Hailey Leavitt. The mother's an exec at Kraft and the sister appears to have gone off the grid." He looked at his watch. "I better hit the shower. What are you going to do about clients?"

"What day is it? Wednesday? I'm in luck. No clients today." Her client load fluctuated from month to month, and she'd recently had a flurry of terminations. She usually started biting her nails when her practice slowed to a dribble, but this time she was glad it had taken a dip.

She went to her desk in the bedroom to check her calendar. *Only six sessions left for the rest of the week.   Plenty of time to run around looking for suspects.*

"I probably ought to look professional if I'm going to get a grieving mother to let me into her house."   Clad in black jeans, his feet and chest bare, Zach pulled a dress shirt and jacket out of the closet.

Cassidy, seated in her desk chair on the opposite side of the room, gazed admiringly at her husband, not because he was movie-star handsome like Jordan, but because he was solid, reliable, and tough-minded.   Just under six feet, he had broad shoulders and a wide chest, with dark silver-threaded hair, a hawkish nose, and a jagged scar across his left cheek.

Zach finished dressing, then sat at his desk, which stood a few feet from hers, and picked up the cordless.

"Can I listen in?" Cassidy asked.

"Sure."   He punched in numbers.   "This is Zach Moran from the *Post* and I'd like—"

"I'm not talking to reporters."   Ellen Leavitt's voice was thick and clogged with tears.

"Please don't hang up.   Let me explain why you might want to make an exception in my case.   Most of my colleagues will treat your daughter's murder like just another Chicago homicide.   They'll cite her age, profession, and a quote or two from her neighbors.   Some will sensationalize the circumstances surrounding her death.   I think she deserves more.   She was a doctor, a healer.   I'd like to do an in-depth piece focusing on who she was and the tragedy of her death."

"She was a family doctor, not a brain surgeon.   Of course *I* know how special she was, but I'm not sure there's anything I could tell you that would convey"—Cassidy heard a sniffle—"convey that to your readers."

"If I can turn her into a real person, most readers will feel a sense of sadness at her loss."

For several seconds all Cassidy could hear was the sound of ragged breathing. Then, "All right, I'll talk to you. But if I get the impression you're up to something, your butt will be out the door before you can say the word 'reporter.'"

They agreed to meet at Ellen's lakeview high rise at nine.

Zach swiveled toward Cassidy. "You better get ready."

She tilted her head to one side. "You sounded like you meant what you said about making Claudia into a real person."

"I always sound like I mean what I say."

"A lot of the time you're just saying whatever you think will work. But this time you sounded genuine."

Zach shrugged. "It'll be a better story if I can make people feel something."

"So you're doing this for purely cynical reasons."

He gave her a bland smile. "Did I forget to tell you what I do for a living?"

Cassidy tossed her nightshirt on the unmade bed and headed for the bathroom. She didn't believe Zach was just doing his job. She thought that Claudia's murder had gotten to him and that he was more invested in her story than he cared to admit

Chapter 9

Ellen Leavitt opened her condo door partway and stared at Cassidy, a frown forming on her regal, perfectly made-up face.

Cassidy didn't allow the surprise she felt to show. She'd been picturing a mother overwhelmed by grief, a woman who'd thrown on her clothes and barely taken time to run a comb through her hair when she'd gone with the police to identify the body. Instead, Claudia's mother was attired in a softly tailored navy pantsuit and low matching heels, her streaked blond hair stylishly coifed. The only signs of the distress Cassidy had heard in her voice were the red veins in her blurry eyes and a small gold hoop in one ear, nothing in the other.

Ellen turned her gaze on Zach. "You didn't say you were bringing anyone with you."

"Sorry. This is my wife Cassidy. She's doing research for a book about crime victims and she wants to learn as much as she can about your daughter."

Ellen leveled her eyes at Cassidy, her frown deepening. "Claudia would never want to be thought of as a victim. She was very intelligent, very assertive. I can assure you she did nothing to bring this on herself."

Oh yes she did. She didn't run like hell when she encountered men like Jordan.

"Look, I landed in the hospital once when I was mugged and I hate it when people blame the victim. What I want to show is that crime often strikes randomly and no one is immune."

"All right," Ellen said, "you can come in." She stood back and opened the door wider. Then, in a barely audible tone, "I just hope I don't live to regret it."

"Neither Cass nor I have any interest in taking advantage of you. Or of making Claudia look bad, either."

Ellen nodded and they moved on into the living room. In front of them a wide arched window overlooked Lake Michigan. Cassidy gazed out at diamond-edged splinters of light reflecting off the choppy surface of the gray-green water. Near the window stood a rectangular wooden coffee table holding two glossy books, a colorful glass bird, and an outsized chess board with elaborately carved marble pieces. A green and gold striped loveseat stood on one side of the table, two green wingback chairs on the other.

Ellen waved toward the chairs. Cassidy and Zach each took one, and Ellen lowered herself onto the loveseat.

"God," she said, "I don't know what's the matter with me. I almost offered you a glass of wine and it's only"—she glanced at her Rolex—"a few minutes after nine. I've been up so long...this day seems to be going on forever."

Zach took a notepad out of his inner jacket pocket. "After what you've been through, a glass of wine might be in order."

Ellen straightened her back. "I never drink before five."

"It must've been such a shock, finding a policeman at your door in the wee hours," Cassidy said.

"I kept telling him he was wrong. That it couldn't be Claudia because she was out of town."

"You thought she was out of town?" Zach asked.

"She called last week...I don't know what day it was...said she was going on vacation. She planned to leave Saturday morning and be gone a week. So she shouldn't have been anywhere near—."

Ellen's cell phone burbled a short piece of music that sounded vaguely familiar. She pulled it out of her pants pocket, checked the caller I.D., and answered in a voice that turned instantly crisp and businesslike. "Whoever told you I was working from home got it wrong...Of course I know how much pressure...Why can't Hernandez review it? All right, fax it over, but I can't promise to get to it today."

While Ellen talked on the phone, Zach scribbled notes on his pad.

"What are you writing?" Ellen demanded as she slipped her cell back into her pocket.

"What you said about Claudia's vacation plans."

"You can't use that! It'll sound like she lied to me."

"I won't quote you on it," Zach said, "but if someone else tells me the same thing, I'll include it in my story."

Cassidy asked in a soft voice, "Do you think she was lying to you?"

Ellen shook her head. "She'd have no reason to. We don't talk that much. It's just that we're both so busy—constantly on the go. She could've been out of town for weeks and I wouldn't have known...Maybe she changed her mind and didn't tell me."

But if she wanted her mother to think *she was gone when she wasn't, she'd have to lie.*

Zach asked, "Where did she plan to go?"

"She intended to head east and see what happened. Her life at home is so structured. She wanted her trip to be as spontaneous as possible. She was going to turn off her cell and not take any electronic devices so nobody could get in touch with her." Ellen leaned forward and moved a bishop so that it stood exactly in the center of its square. "I suppose she could have gotten tired of driving and come home early."

"You think that's what she did?" Cassidy asked.

"It doesn't seem like her. Claudia always knew what she wanted. She didn't start off to do something and then change her mind."

"And you don't think she would have let you know if she shortened her trip?"

Ellen stared at a point beyond Cassidy's left shoulder. "I told you we didn't talk often. If she called anybody, it would have been Jill. That's the nurse who works at her office."

"Why Jill?" Zach asked.

"She's Claudia's best friend. Claudia isn't— wasn't the type to go around baring her soul, but if she confided in anybody, it would've been Jill."

"Isn't it unusual for doctors and nurses to be so close?" Zach shifted in his chair.

"Claudia roomed with Jill her first couple of years in premed. Then Jill ran into some financial problems and decided to switch to nursing."

"I understand Claudia has—"Cassidy was interrupted by Ellen's cell. Ellen stood and paced in a tight circle while she talked to someone from her office. After about a minute, she put her phone away and sat down again. "Sorry. What were you saying?"

"I wanted to know if Claudia got along with her sister?"

A shuttered expression came over Ellen's face. "I suppose you got your information about our family from the Net."

"LexisNexis," Zach said. "It's standard procedure for journalists to look up the family members of a murder victim."

"Yes, of course." Ellen looked over Cassidy's shoulder again. "Hailey's six years younger. She and Claudia didn't have much in common. I'd have to say they were estranged."

"Hailey probably doesn't know anything but I'd still like to ask her a couple of questions," Zach said. "Could you give me her number?"

"I'd rather you didn't talk to her. Claudia and I were the strong ones. Hailey always took things harder than we did. Even though they didn't stay in touch, I'm sure Claudia's murder will throw Hailey into a tailspin. The last thing she needs is a reporter and his wife asking intrusive questions."

Ooooh. I don't think she likes us any more.

"I'm sorry," Zach said. "I didn't mean to get too personal."

The stiffness in Ellen's shoulders eased a little. "It's probably just me. It makes me nervous, talking to a reporter. I don't want the details of Claudia's private life—or mine either—to show up in the *Post*."

Wants to keep her private life private? Avoiding publicity instead of plastering pictures of herself all over the Web? How quaint.

"I'm not out to embarrass anybody," Zach said.

Cassidy added, "What we're both looking for is a sense of who Claudia was. What did you love most about her? What were her passions? Her pet peeves?"

"What did I love most...?" Ellen cocked her head. "Her dedication to her patients. I really admired that in her. She always wanted to help people. I think it went back to the time when her father was dying. She was only eleven but she'd sit by his bed for hours." Ellen paused. "Oh, and here's another thing. I loved the sound of her laughter. She had this sunny disposition and was always upbeat, even when her life was very difficult."

"When was it difficult?"

"Well...when she was in medical school, of course."

Cassidy narrowed her eyes, wondering if Ellen Leavitt didn't know about the order of protection, or just didn't want to talk about it.

"What about her passions?" Cassidy asked.

"She loved to dance. You should have seen her. It was like her feet never touched the floor. And nature. Whenever she had time, she'd find some trail to hike. And then there was poetry. When she was a kid, she collected all her favorite poems and made them into a book." Ellen's watery eyes filled with tears.

"She sounds like a wonderful person," Cassidy said. "But what about pet peeves? Everybody's got them."

"I wish I knew her better. I wish we'd gone shopping and had lunch. The only thing I can think of is, she disliked people who put themselves first. She was so self-sacrificing. She couldn't understand people who didn't give as much as she did."

Ellen dabbed beneath her eyes with one finger, apparently trying to do the least possible damage to her makeup. "I'm sorry, but this has been exhausting. I need to lie down for a while. So if you'll excuse me...."

Lie down? Take off her suit and wash off her makeup? I don't think so.

Chapter 10

Zach paid twenty dollars to retrieve his Subaru from a parking garage two blocks west of Ellen's Oak Street high rise. Drawing up to the curb in the nearest no parking zone, he took his notepad out of one pocket, his cell phone out of another.

"Jill?"

"Yeah."

"How'd you get her number?"

"I'm calling Claudia's office. If Jill isn't there, I'll grab my laptop out of the trunk and use LexisNexis to get her home number."

While Zach dialed, Cassidy gazed across the street at a Gothic church being rehabbed for condos. In every corner of the city, old buildings were being recycled or torn down and new construction was going up. *More housing for yuppies, less for the poor.*

She fished a notepad of her own out of her purse and began writing down what they'd learned from Ellen. She did the same with client records. She never took notes in front of them because it broke the rapport.

Zach spoke into his cell. "Is Jill there?" A long pause. "This is Zach Moran from the *Post*. I'm researching a story on Dr. Leavitt's murder and I'd like to talk to you...Today if possible...Harvey's at twelve-fifteen? I'll be there. Oh, and I'm bringing my wife. She's working on a book about crime victims." He ended his call.

"Jill certainly didn't require persuading."

"Once I say I'm from the *Post*, most people can't wait to spill their guts. Even though it's only print and not broadcast."

Cassidy checked her watch. "We've got a lot of time to kill."

"I know a bar that opens at ten."

"I'm sure you do."

"My stomach's growling. Let's drive to Uptown where there's street parking and have breakfast at a greasy spoon."

As they headed north on Lake Shore Drive, Cassidy said, "After talking to Ellen, there are two things I want to find out. One is, what's the side of Claudia that's not so saintly?"

Zach chimed in, "And the other is, why is Ellen so anxious to keep us away from Hailey?"

Cassidy made a face at him. "Where's the mystery in having a husband who finishes your paragraphs?"

Cassidy and Zach sat in a vinyl booth at Harvey's waiting for Jill to walk through the dirt-streaked glass door. Cassidy glanced at the other patrons. Two beat cops huddled over green salads. Three thickset women, one wearing white socks and runover gym shoes beneath a gathered skirt, discussed their favorite soaps. An elderly man with a long scraggly beard sipped from a coffee mug.

A willowy dark-haired woman came through the door. Zach stood and waved her over to their booth.

"Zach Moran?" she asked.

"Right." He gestured toward Cassidy, who was still seated. "This is my wife, Cass McCabe. She's a psychotherapist, and she's worked with some people who were crime victims, which inspired her to write a book."

As Jill slid onto the bench seat, Zach sat down again. The nurse had a crop of wild curly hair pinned back from a face that was slightly too narrow for her broad features. She was model thin and far more stylishly dressed than Cassidy. Her splotchy skin and puffy eyes indicated that she had been crying.

"I appreciate your taking the time to meet with us," Zach began.

"I'm sorry I couldn't think of anyplace better than Harvey's. This is where I always come for lunch and my brain's flaked out on me today. The ambience stinks but the desserts are to die for."

"You don't look like you ever touch dessert," Cassidy observed.

"I wish. Claudia was always after me to eat healthy, but I love food, especially sweets, and I could never restrain myself. I was so fat in high school the only boy I could get dates with wore a pocket protector. I kid you not. He really had one. But I'm talking too much. Whenever I'm stressed, I can't stop babbling."

That's a good thing. Babblers are easier to extract information from.

"So how do you eat all you want and stay thin?"

You should be offering condolences instead of talking about food.

But I need to know. When my metabolism slows down, my Reese's habit will lead to plus-size shopping.

"I exercise at the health club an hour before work. Every day of the week. And I gotta tell you, I hate exercising. But it's the only way I can eat all I want and still keep my weight down."

Cassidy, never able to make herself exercise, propped her cheek on her hand. "You can't stop eating sweets but you can force yourself to exercise?"

"Weird, isn't it? It's like I got so sick of being fat I developed this Nazi part that cracks the whip and makes me do whatever I have to to get thin."

A blond, pony-tailed teenager wearing jeans and a stained *Harvey's* tee shirt over small jiggly breasts came to take their orders. Zach's gaze lingered for a moment on the girl's bosom, then moved to her bored face. Cassidy understood that men liked to look and that his appreciation of other women's attributes had nothing to do with his feelings for her. As long as he was discreet about it, his glances didn't bother her.

The girl stood next to their table, one bony hip jutting out, and asked what they wanted. Jill ordered a philly cheese steak sandwich and a Dr. Pepper. Zach ordered a hamburger and coffee. Kicking him under the table because they'd eaten large breakfasts a little over an hour earlier, Cassidy virtuously ordered iced tea.

Zach looked at Jill. "We talked to Ellen Leavitt this morning and she told us you were Claudia's best friend."

Chapter 11

"I know," Jill replied, her demeanor turning somber. "Ellen called and asked me not to tell you about the problems between Claudia and her. Ever since we talked, I've been trying to decide what to do." Jill peered at Zach. "You said you were researching a story. What does that mean?"

"I'm trying to find out as much as I can about Claudia. From what I've heard so far, I have the impression she was an outstanding person—maybe even inspirational. I know everyone has their faults, but I'm not looking to tarnish her reputation. I just want to write a story about a good person who devoted herself to helping others and was brutally murdered."

Jill shot Zach a skeptical look. "If you came across a juicy piece of gossip, I can't believe you wouldn't put it in your story."

"Depends. If it was connected to her murder, I'd use it. Otherwise, I leave gossip to the tabloids."

"I Googled you and found out that you and your wife have solved a few murders. Are you investigating this one?"

"If I run across any leads, I'll see where they take me. But I have a hunch the police already have the most likely suspect in custody."

Cassidy winced.

"You mean that creep who was harassing her?"

Zach nodded.

The waitress plunked plates and glasses down in front of them. Jill squirted a wiggly line of ketchup across her fries. Cassidy swished her straw in her iced tea and thought about where to begin.

Start with something easy. Then, when her guard is down, circle around to the conflict between Claudia and her mother.

Cassidy took a napkin out of its metal holder and set it beneath her sweating glass. "Ellen told us Claudia was supposed to be out of town. Was that your understanding as well?"

"She'd been talking about her vacation for weeks. Told us all good-bye last Friday. She was supposed to be completely out of touch until this coming Monday. Kelly and I—she's our med tech—can't make any sense of it. We have no idea what she was doing home yesterday."

Cassidy asked, "Had she ever been on a vacation like this before?"

"No, but it was just the sort of thing she'd do. Me, I'd have to plan everything out ahead of time and I'd never go by myself. But Claudia had this spirit of adventure. She was the most independent person I know. The only aspect of her job she ever complained about was that every minute of her time was scheduled."

Zach jotted something in his notepad. "You think she might have told everybody she was going to be gone so nobody'd bother her and then used the week to hole up with some boyfriend?"

Jill waved a ketchup-smeared french fry in the air. "Well, she did have a mystery man in her life. But if she was going to spend a week with him, she wouldn't have lied to me about it. She never felt a need to hide things."

Cassidy said, "But if she had a mystery man, she *was* hiding something."

Jill shook her head. "Couple months ago she said she was dating someone new but he didn't want anybody to know about it. It was the guy who wanted to keep it a secret, not Claudia."

Cassidy sucked up some iced tea, then swished her straw again. "You think he's married?"

Jill shrugged.

Loquacious Jill doesn't have anything to say? I'd guess that means Claudia didn't rule men out on the basis of their marriage certificates.

The nurse squinted in thought. "The main reason she wouldn't stay in town without telling anyone is that some of her patients are pretty sick and she'd want to know if any of them went into crisis."

"Wouldn't she want to know that even if she was on the road?"

"If she was far enough away, she couldn't come running to the rescue. I'd guess going incommunicado was the only way she could get a total break from feeling like she was always on call."

A slice of tomato fell out of the hamburger Zach was holding in both hands. He said, "Okay, let's assume she left town on Saturday and returned Tuesday without telling anyone. Can you think of any reason she'd do that?"

Jill shook her head, a perplexed look on her face.

"Maybe driving around the country wasn't as much fun as she thought it would be," Cassidy said. "Maybe she got lonely or bored or had car trouble."

"I suppose it's possible but it doesn't seem like her. And I would have expected her to call me if she came home early." Jill twisted one of the many rings on her right hand. "Although obviously she *was* home and she didn't let me know."

"Were you two the kind of friends who told each other everything?"

"I'd say we were pretty close...although I have to admit, there were some things Claudia kept to herself."

"I thought you said she didn't hide anything."

"That's not what I meant. It was just that she was self-sufficient and didn't need to go around blabbing about everything the way I do."

Zach stuffed the last bite of hamburger into his mouth. He chewed and swallowed, then said, "Didn't she share the office with another doc?"

"Paul Goldstein. He's a good guy. Claudia wouldn't have partnered with him if he wasn't."

Cassidy asked, "Can you think of anybody who might've wanted to hurt her? Besides the guy she took out the order against?"

Jill's animated face went flat. "Everyone loved her."

Somebody may have loved her too much.

"It sounds like the only person she didn't get along with was her mother."

Jill stared out the window for several seconds. "Okay, I'll tell you. But first we need to order dessert." She beckoned to the young waitress, who sauntered over to their table and began clearing dishes.

Jill ordered a slice of chocolate caramel cheesecake.

"Can I get chocolate cake with chocolate ice cream?" Cassidy asked.

The girl nodded and wrote it down.

"Just coffee for me," Zach said.

Jill looked at her watch. "Jeeze, I'm going to be late. Oh well, they'll just have to get along without me for a while." She gazed out the window again. "The problems between Claudia and her mother started when Claudia's father got cancer. Before that, Ellen was Super Mom. You know the type—

baked cookies with the kids, took them to story hour at the library, gave them gobs of attention. Then after he died, they had no source of income and Ellen panicked. She'd always been there for the kids and then suddenly she wasn't there at all. So Claudia had to step up and take care of her little sister."

The waitress brought their desserts and Zach's coffee.

A blissful look came over Jill's face as she savored her first bite of cheesecake. Cassidy loaded up her fork, relishing the cool sensation of ice cream melting in her mouth.

"How old were the kids when they lost their dad?" she asked.

"Let's see...." Jill's brow furrowed. "I think Claudia was eleven and Hailey was five. So anyway, Ellen spent a few months wringing her hands, then went to work for Kraft and took classes at night to get her MBA. That left Claudia to take over the cookie baking."

"So she basically raised her sister."

"Back then she was happy to do it. It made her feel like a grown up, and she loved the sense of being needed by Hailey and her mom."

Zach folded his arms on the table. "So what went wrong?"

"Hailey." Jill's mouth tightened. "She went into middle school, started running with a wild crowd, and got completely out of control. That's when Claudia decided that being a surrogate mom wasn't all it was cracked up to be. She kept after Ellen to impose some discipline, and Ellen did make some attempts, but she didn't do nearly enough to satisfy Claudia. In my opinion, at that point there wasn't much she could do."

Cassidy waited a moment before taking another bite, wanting her dessert to last as long as possible. "It must've killed Claudia to watch the child she'd raised get in trouble like that."

"She told me that for years she thought it was her fault. But then she started seeing a counselor when she went to college and came to realize that she was too young to be saddled with so much responsibility. So she mentally flipped it and started blaming her mother instead."

"Is that why Claudia kept her mother at arm's length?"

"You haven't heard the half of it."

Chapter 12

Jill finished her Dr. Pepper and set the glass down with an angry thump. "Hailey moved in with her boyfriend and had a baby when she was sixteen. The only thing that girl ever did right was to not take drugs while she was pregnant. She gave birth to a healthy baby boy named David. He's about fifteen now."

"She kept the baby?" Zach asked.

"Less than a year after David was born, Claudia went to visit and found the poor kid smeared with his own poop and not moving very much. Hailey was so high she could barely get out a coherent sentence. Claudia called DCFS from Hailey's apartment and refused to leave until a worker showed up. She was in her first year of med school at the time. She begged her mother to take the baby so she wouldn't have to drop out, but Ellen was moving up in her career and said she couldn't give David the care he needed. So Claudia felt she had no choice but to quit school and take the baby herself."

"What an incredible person." Zach waved away the waitress who was approaching with a pot of coffee.

"Well, she didn't do it all on her own," Jill said, a defensive note creeping into her voice. "She and I were roomies in premed. Then I decided I didn't want to spend so many years in school—or rack up the debt that went with it—and I switched to nursing. So when Claudia took custody of David, she asked me to help. She didn't want to leave him with a babysitter because she was sure he'd been damaged by all those months with a dopehead mother. We got an apartment together and worked it out so she could be with David during the day while I was in school, then I could be with him at night while she waited tables. It was almost like we were co-parents."

"You really were a good friend to her," Cassidy said.

Jill smiled a wobbly little smile. "Sometimes it was hard, but David was such a sweet little kid it was worth it. And they only lived with me two years. When he turned three, Claudia had him evaluated by a psychologist. The shrink said he'd probably always have some abandonment issues, but he was doing well enough that Claudia could put him in an all-day preschool. She got him into the best one possible, made Ellen pay for it, then went back to school herself."

Cassidy scraped the bottom of her plate, trying to capture every last crumb of ice-cream soaked cake. From what Jordan had told her, she was certain David was no longer living with Claudia when they met. "How long did she have custody?"

"Up until two years ago. Unfortunately, Hailey got clean and the court sent David back to live with her." Disgust swept over Jill's face. "It was horrible."

"God, I hate stories like that," Cassidy said. "Talk about abandonment. Claudia was the only mother the boy had ever known."

"You got that right. Hailey hardly ever visited him and she was high half the time when she did. David and Claudia had this great bond. So then he gets ripped away from the mother he loves and has to go live with the mother who couldn't be bothered to visit. Not only that, but Hailey absolutely loathed her sister for taking David away. I'm sure she badmouths Claudia to the kid every chance she gets. And the other thing he lost was his middle class lifestyle. He got yanked out of a good school in a good neighborhood and dumped into a shitty apartment in Stone Park."

"Sounds pretty rough." Holding up his hands, Zach wrote in the air to signal that he wanted the bill.

Jill said, "Claudia was terrified he'd join a gang or start using as a way to deal with his loss, but they emailed each other all the time and she was fairly sure he was doing okay."

"Can you give me Hailey's phone number?" Zach held his pen over his pad.

"I don't have a clue where she is now."

"Would Ellen know?"

"I couldn't say."

"What about David's email address?"

Jill shook her head. "I hate to admit it, but I didn't stay in touch."

The teenager dropped their bill on the table, then spun on her heels, her ponytail swirling out around her.

Zach said, "The other person I'd like to talk to is the doctor she shares her office with. What are the chances of his giving us an interview?"

"He'll probably say yes. I'll check with him and get back to you."

"Thanks." Zach fished a business card out of his wallet, added a couple of numbers, and handed it to Jill.

"I ran way over my thirty-minute lunch break but nobody's going to care today."

"When was the last time you saw her?" Cassidy asked softly.

Jill covered her mouth with her hand and looked away. Grabbing a paper napkin, she blew her nose, then replied, "Friday evening. I told her to be sure to do everything I wouldn't while she was away. When I left, she was the only one still in the office. Catching up on paperwork before her trip."

Jill walked through the door ahead of them while Zach stopped at the cash register to pay. Out on the sidewalk, Cassidy raised a hand to shield her eyes from the glare as she watched Jill move rapidly away from them. April sunshine streamed down from a vivid blue sky, but the rays brought more light than heat. Cassidy wished she'd worn a heavier jacket.

"Where's Claudia's office?"

"Couple blocks south of here. We'll drive past it on our way to Hyde Park."

"Why are we going there?"

"To find out if any of her neighbors saw her during the time she was supposed to be away."

They climbed into the Subaru and drove to the north end of the block. Cassidy gazed out at a faded *Welcome to Edgewater* banner on a lamp post, orange plastic palm trees in front of a car wash, rusted parking meters, and a brown-skinned mother pushing a child in a rickety stroller.

Zach hung a U-turn and cruised back in the direction Jill was walking. A short distance from Harvey's the neighborhood changed from seedy to medium chic, with boutiques, coffee shops, and antique stores crammed along both sides of the street.

"Claudia's office is in the middle of this block on the right," Zach said.

Cassidy spotted a green canopy printed with white letters: Edgewater Family Practice. "A mixed neighborhood. What a perfect fit. Enough patients with insurance to pay off her student loans, enough without to indulge her do-gooder side."

"She wouldn't lack for pro bono work here."

Cassidy fingered a loose thread on the sleeve of her jacket. "Jill certainly delivered up an earful."

"All we had to do was ply her with cheesecake."

"The thing that caught my attention was the mystery man. If the guy was married and Claudia threatened to tell his wife, that would give *him* a motive. Or if the wife found out, that would give *her* a motive."

"I can't picture a woman creating a crime scene like that," Zach said. "Everything about it—the clothing tossed around the room, the naked body in the bed—bore the stamp of an enraged lover."

"A woman could have set it up to make it look like the killer was a man."

"There aren't a lot of women strong enough to carry a body up a flight of stairs."

Cassidy took out her notepad and filled several pages with the information they had gleaned from Jill.

Chapter 13

Zach pulled up in front of Claudia's graystone. To the right stood a brick Tudor with a tall chimney, dormers, and limestone ornamentation. To the left stood a nondescript two-story frame with a wide front porch. A Honda was parked in the driveway of the frame house.

"Good chance somebody's home over there." Zach nodded toward the car.

He pressed the doorbell, waited thirty seconds, and pressed again.

"The owner could have taken public transportation," Cassidy ventured, knowing Zach held a firm belief that people would eventually open doors if he harassed them long enough.

He continued ringing the bell.

Cassidy shifted from one foot to the other, wondering how long she would be stuck on the porch before he gave up. *Don't be so negative. Zach usually does get people to answer.*

After about five minutes—an excruciating length of time for Cassidy—the door opened half an inch and a woman's gravelly voice said, "Go away!"

"I'm a reporter from the *Post*. I need to talk to you."

"You're too late. I've already talked to all the cops and reporters I'm going to."

"This is important. You don't want an inaccurate story about Dr. Leavitt to show up in the *Post*, do you?"

"You should've been out here at the crack of dawn like everybody else."

"I thought it would be easier on the neighbors if I didn't shout questions at them in the middle of the uproar."

"Oh fuck!"

Cassidy heard the metallic click of a chain being released.   The door opened wider, revealing a woman in her forties wearing a ratty robe and slippers, her short sandy hair almost as colorless as her pale, truculent face.   With nearly invisible brows and lashes, her round countenance appeared cartoonish.

This woman should never step foot off the funny pages without applying a heavy coat of makeup.

"First I hear sirens in the middle of the night, then I go stand outside with some of the other neighbors and we're hoping against hope the medics will bring her out on a gurney.   Time keeps going by and they don't, and then"—the woman's voice broke—"then we see them carrying out a body bag.   And after that, the reporters swarm around me and I can barely talk."   She hugged herself. "Then I have to get my daughter up, feed her, drive her to school.   When I get home, I call in to have my graduate student take my classes today.   I just sit in bed shaking for a while and finally I calm down enough to go to sleep.   Then you start ringing my goddamn bell and just keep ringing and won't stop."

"I can see why you're angry," Cassidy said, feeling a pang of guilt.

"Sorry I got you up," Zach said.   "The reason I need to talk to you is, I understand Dr. Leavitt was a dedicated, self-sacrificing person and I want my story to do her justice.   I didn't think the piece would be complete without talking to at least one of her neighbors."

"Oh fuck.   I'm not going to get back to sleep anyway so I might as well answer your damn questions."

Zach introduced himself and Cassidy and gave the writing-a-book explanation.

"Madison Ferris." She led the way into a room with plants hanging in front of the windows and a shelving unit filled with primitive wooden statues. They all sat down.

Leaning slightly forward, Zach took out his pad. "I've talked to a couple of people who said Dr. Leavitt was supposed to be out of town all week. Do you have any idea why she was at home last night?"

"I thought you were going to write about how dedicated and self-sacrificing she was."

"I am. But I also have to try and come up with an answer to this odd little mystery regarding her whereabouts. Did she talk to you about her trip?"

"She told me about it last week when we got together for a glass of wine. In fact, that's the reason she invited me over. She didn't want me to worry if I didn't see her around. Not that I would. I'm way too busy to pay attention to her comings and goings. But she was always thoughtful like that." Madison rubbed the back of her index finger against her nostrils.

"What did she say about her trip?" Cassidy asked.

"Just that she was going to be gone a week. I offered to take in the mail and feed her cat, but she said she'd already hired someone to do it."

Claudia had a cat? Hope it's not locked up in her house without food and water.

"To tell the truth," Madison continued, "I was relieved. What with taking care of my daughter and all the hours I put in at the University, there are nights when it's all I can do to fix cereal for dinner."

"You must be really overloaded."

"You can say that again. The only reason I offered is that I owed her for the times she came over at night to check on Kristi when she was sick. I was so grateful not to have to take her to the ER."

"You and Claudia must've been pretty good friends," Cassidy remarked.

"I guess you could say that." Madison's face scrunched up. She grabbed a tissue out of her pocket, turned her head away, and exploded in a fit of sneezes. Then she vigorously blew her nose. "Allergies."

Zach tapped his pen against his pad. "You were telling us about your friendship with Dr. Leavitt."

"Sometimes we'd get together in the evening and she'd tell me about her love life and I'd tell her about the joys"—Madison made quotation marks in the air—"of single motherhood. Not that she didn't know already, having practically raised her nephew. But we didn't see that much of each other because she had this bad habit of falling in love." Madison grimaced. "You're not going to use that, are you?"

"We can go off the record if you like. That means—"

"I know what it means. You won't use what I tell you, but now that I've clued you in, you'll sniff around until you find someone willing to talk about her love life *on* the record."

Zach gave her his bland smile. "You have a good grasp of the news biz."

"Getting back to her trip," Cassidy said, "did you see the person she hired to feed her cat?"

"Yeah, a couple of times. A teenaged boy in one of those hoody things."

"I keep wondering if she might have wanted everybody to think she was out of town when her real agenda was to stay home and attend to something she didn't want anybody to know about."

"That's nuts. Claudia was extremely open. Not the type to carry out a charade like that at all.

Besides, Kristi and I saw her leave. Kristi went over early Saturday morning to help Claudia pack, then we both stood on the porch and waved good-bye."

Chapter 14

Out on the sidewalk, Zach walked purposefully toward the Tudor on the other side of Claudia's house. Cassidy reluctantly trailed behind him.

Zach's never the least bit abashed about knocking on doors, but you hate it. Makes you feel like a vacuum cleaner salesman.

While he stood on the porch ringing the bell, Cassidy paused on the walkway to admire the place next door. It was about half the width of the other houses on the block, a two-story, ivy-covered red brick dwelling with a steeply pitched roof and an arched door. *Looks like a fairy tale cottage. The kind of place Goldilocks might've stumbled across in the woods.* The yard was surrounded by a short picket fence. Various desiccated flora that hadn't greened out yet covered the ground. Red and yellow tulips provided a splash of color, with tiny brick paths curving amidst the plants. Cassidy noticed a concrete dwarf peeking out from the vegetation. Looking more closely, she spotted three more, each standing or sitting in a different position. *Gotta be seven in all. And this domain belongs to Sleeping Beauty, not Goldilocks.*

Before long, Zach gave up on his bell-ringing and came to join her. "I don't have time to keep this up."

"Oh, what a shame. I was so looking forward to hitting every house on the block."

He smiled. "I'm sure you were."

Looking past Zach, Cassidy noticed a woman with a dog moving toward them on the sidewalk. "Here comes somebody."

They went to meet her. As tall as Zach, she wore two pullovers and a shapeless cardigan over baggy corduroy pants. She had wispy white hair and a deeply wrinkled face, but she moved along briskly. At the end of her leash trotted a black dog about the size of a lab, with long shaggy hair.

Zach said, "I'm a reporter for the *Post* and I'd like to ask some questions."

She gave him a blank look. The dog tried to poke its nose in Cassidy's crotch but she fended him off. *Cats may be aloof but at least they have no interest in smelling your private parts.*

Zach showed the sweater lady his press pass. "I'm working on a story about your neighbor, Claudia Leavitt. Did you know her?"

"I think that's her place over there." The woman pointed at the gray stone. "I might've met her a few times. I live in that house on the corner." She thrust her thumb backward, indicating an unkempt bungalow at the end of the block.

The dog suddenly bounded toward a squirrel, nearly dragging the woman off her feet. Zach grabbed her shoulders to keep her from falling. Reaching the end of its leash, the dog jerked to a stop and let loose with a volley of barks.

"Heel, Duffy."

Duffy gave his human a mournful look, barked once more, then went to sit at her feet.

Of course, to be perfectly fair, cats don't obey either.

Cassidy touched the woman's arm. "Did you know Claudia died last night?"

"She did?" The woman gazed vaguely at Cassidy. "Claudia's yard always looks so nice. My yard used to look nice too when my husband was alive. But now that he's gone, it's too much for me. You'd think my kids would give me a hand but they always say they're too busy. They want to stick me in a nursing home. Well, forget them. I've lived in that house over forty years and I'm not leaving till they carry me out feet first."

"I don't blame you," Cassidy said. "I wouldn't want to live in a nursing home either."

"We're investigating Claudia's death," Zach said. "Did you notice anything unusual on the block in the past week or so? Anybody who didn't belong?"

"Unusual?" Her brow creased. "I don't think so." She bent over to pat Duffy's head, eliciting a soft doggie moan. "Well, there was that car. I take Duffy for a walk around six in the morning and a couple times I saw a car parked near my house with a man in it. Couldn't figure out why anybody'd be just sitting in his car."

"Can you tell me what the man looked like?"

"Just normal."

"What about the car?"

"A sedan. Some dark color. I didn't really pay attention."

"Was there anything unusual about the car or the man?"

"Not really. Except I didn't like his bumper sticker. It had a dirty word in it."

Cassidy asked, "Which dirty word?"

"The F word. 'F the pigs.'"

"How long ago did you see the car? Was it in the past five days?"

"Mighta been."

"Thanks," Zach said. "You've been very helpful."

"I can't stay out here any longer. He wants meat and potatoes every single day and he likes to eat early. I'm so sick of cooking. I wish he'd settle for soup and a sandwich once in a while." The sweater lady started back toward her house.

"Who is it you have to cook for?" Cassidy called after her.

"My old man, of course."

Zach took Cassidy's hand and they walked in the direction of the Subaru. "Here I thought we had something. A dude doing surveillance on Claudia's house. But the car's probably about as real as the meat-and-potatoes husband."

"There's no way to tell. People with dementia mix up truth and fiction."

"I'm with her kids. That woman belongs in a nursing home."

"What if Gran got a little dotty? Would you want to send her off to a nursing home?" Cassidy's grandmother brought cheer into the lives of everybody who knew her.

"Don't even say such a thing."

"Well, that old lady we just talked to couldn't go into a nursing home. They don't take dogs and she'd never leave Duffy."

Talking about the dog reminded Cassidy that Madison had told them about a recently orphaned animal. "What's going to happen to Claudia's cat?"

"Animal control's already taken it to the pound."

"Maybe we could—"

Zach gave her his are-you-nuts stare. "Here we are in the middle of a murder investigation and you want to try to rescue this one cat when thousands get put to sleep every year because there're more of them than there are people willing to take them."

"Yes, but...." *So what's your plan? Starshine won't tolerate any family expansions—especially not four-legged ones. And you don't know a soul who's looking to adopt.*

"Okay," she said. "And I want you to note, sometimes I do listen to reason."

Chapter 15

Zach's phone rang while he was inserting his key into the ignition. He answered, then listened for a while. "Hey, Jill, thanks for setting it up." He put his cell back in his pocket.

"The doctor agreed to see us?"

"Dr. Paul Goldstein. We're meeting him at the clinic at five. In the meantime, I have to get over to Area One and convince one of the dicks I know to leak a description of the crime scene so I can attribute it to an anonymous police source. I'll take you to one of the commercial streets and put you in a cab so you can go on home. Then I'll swing around later and pick you up so we can get to the clinic by five."

"I'll jump on the el."

The line that ran from the base of Zach's nose to his jaw deepened. "Look, we're not about to go on food stamps. Make it easy on yourself and take the damn cab."

Having grown up with wealth, Zach had been trying to liberate Cassidy from her poverty mindset ever since they got married. She'd made considerable progress, but cabs still seemed an unnecessary indulgence. *Yes, but you're not sure how to get home from here and Zach's not comfortable with you traveling through the infamous south side on an el.*

"Okay, I'll take the cab."

Cassidy and Zach returned to the far northside neighborhood where the clinic was located. They walked in the door at twenty to five. A man sat in a chair reading a newspaper. *Evidently the doc hasn't gotten to his last patient yet. Well, what doctor ever does run on time? Especially on a day when he learned his partner was murdered.*

They parked themselves at the end of the row of chairs the man was occupying. A woman wearing a tight neon blue shirt sat at a monitor behind a long counter.

Cassidy picked up a magazine touting an article on how to improve your sex life. Skimming the text, she was gratified to discover that she and Zach were ahead of the curve. The only recommended position they hadn't tried was in the shower. She suppressed a laugh as a picture formed in her head.

Jill came through a doorway next to the counter and greeted them. "Things have been crazy here today but he should be able to see you in about half an hour." She returned to the interior part of the office.

A few minutes later a plump woman burst into the room and marched up to the counter. She didn't actually burst, but she emitted so much nervous energy it seemed as if she had. She said to the woman in the blue top, "You tell Dr. Goldstein that Gwen Dickert is here to see him."

Cassidy stared at the well-upholstered woman with the demanding voice. She looked to be in her thirties, with straight, dishwater blond hair brushing her shoulders and a cross hanging around her neck. She wore a long knit tunic and matching pants that had seen better days. Her face was twisted into a scowl.

Blue Top said, "Doctor is with a patient and I don't see your name on the appointment list. Perhaps you have the wrong day?"

"I don't need an appointment to let him know what I think of him. You tell him if he doesn't have the balls to face me, I'm gonna throw the biggest hissy fit anybody around here's ever seen."

Blue Top stood and squared her shoulders. "You'll have to wait till he comes out of the exam room.   When he does, I'll give him the message." She turned and started toward the inner office, but before she'd taken more than two steps, a young male breezed through the doorway next to the counter, followed by a trim man in a lab coat.

"Bye, Dr. Goldstein." The young guy waved and left the clinic.

"Hello, Gwen," the doctor said.

Plowing toward him, she cried out, "You killed my mother!"

The doctor's head and shoulders reared back as if she'd hit him.   For an instant the room was silent.   Then he drew himself up and spoke.   "I realize this is a difficult time, but I'm not responsible for your mother's death. You need to take a deep breath and calm yourself down."

"Don't tell me to calm down!"   Gwen's voice sounded even more agitated than before.   "I'm not calming down till you admit what you did."

"I can't discuss your mother's case in front of all these people.   If you want to talk about it, we'll set up an appointment and you can come back later."

"We're going to talk about it now.   I want all these people to hear how you killed her so they'll know what kind of doctor you are."

His face turned ashen.   His eyes darted around the room as if looking for a way out.   "Your mother's case is confidential.   Please come back into my office where we can talk privately."

"I'm not taking one step till you tell me what you did to her!"

Poor guy. What's he going to do? Probably doesn't want to call the cops. Got this hysterical woman in his face and he can't get rid of her.

Dr. Goldstein stepped close to Gwen and started speaking in a whisper. Cassidy, sitting only a few feet away, strained to hear him.

"I swear, I did nothing to hurt your mother."

"You're lying!" She jabbed a finger at him. "You wrote on the death certificate that she died of a probable heart attack, but a couple months earlier she had an EKG and you told me her heart was perfectly sound."

"I would never have said that. An EKG measures the electric signals that control the rhythm of the heart. It has no predictive value in terms of a heart attack."

"There's no history of heart disease in our family. You knew my mother wanted to die, so you came into our house while we were gone and gave her a shot that killed her."

"I can't discuss this with you now. I have a patient to see."

"You're going to stand right here and listen to what I have to say." She planted her hands on her broad hips. "I always thought I could trust you. You seemed so compassionate. But you killed my mother and that's against the law. I won't rest until I see you go to jail for it."

"When did she die?"

"You don't know? You signed the friggin' death certificate."

"I'm sorry, I can't remember off the top—"

"She passed on Saturday, between noon and nine. The only time my husband and I went out together and left her alone. Now isn't that a coincidence?"

"I spent all afternoon Saturday playing golf in a foursome and immediately after that I attended a dinner party. I didn't get home till after midnight."

"How do you explain why my mother, who was only fifty-eight, who'd never had a single problem with her heart, suddenly died of a heart attack during the one time she was alone in the house?"

"These things happen. Her arteries were probably clogged. We never tested for that."

"Lies! All lies! The M.E. took a blood sample so we'll know the real reason soon enough." Gwen turned on her heel and stomped out the door.

Dr. Goldstein retreated into the inner part of his office.

Chapter 16

Cassidy hurried outside in pursuit of Gwen. She was standing on the sidewalk lighting a cigarette with a trembling hand.

"Why did you follow me?"

"I wanted to hear more about your mother's death."

"What do you care?"

"My name's Cass McCabe and my husband's a reporter. I just wanted to know more about what the doctor did to your mother."

A look of interest came over Gwen's face. "You think your husband might write a story about the doctor killing my mother?"

"He wouldn't be able to unless Dr. Goldstein was arrested."

Gwen took a deep drag, tilted her head back, and blew out smoke through her nostrils. "Filthy habit. My husband gets so mad at me. I actually managed to quit for six months. But now...." Her face settled into deep grooves of pain.

"You said your mother wanted to die."

"It was just awful. First she asked me to help her and I told her straight out that only God has the right to take a life. Then she started begging Dr. Goldstein to do it but I never imagined he would. She was a quadriplegic and couldn't stand being helpless, not being able to do the things she used to. I kept telling her, if only she'd take Jesus into her heart, she'd know the peace that passeth understanding. But she wouldn't listen. I prayed for her every day and I was sure God would eventually bring her into the fold and she'd be saved. The worst thing about her passing now is, she'll never be with us in heaven."

Cassidy cupped her right elbow in her left hand. "Did anybody else know she wanted to die? Maybe it wasn't the doctor."

Gwen shook her head. "She never left the house except when I took her to see Dr. Goldstein."

Oh God, if I had her life I'd want to die too.

"About two weeks ago she said she had a bladder infection and insisted I take her to the doctor. Usually I go into the exam room with her but this time she made me wait outside. That's when they cooked it up, I'm sure of it. Me and my husband, we set it up so one or the other of us was always with her. But when Mom went to see the doctor that last time, she knew we were planning to go together to a wedding in Crystal Lake on Saturday. So she told the doctor when she'd be alone and where we hid the key and he came in and killed her."

Gwen looked around vaguely, then dropped her smoke on the sidewalk and ground it out with her heel. Bending over, she picked up the butt. "I have to put this in the garbage. It makes me so mad when people litter."

"So the reason you think Dr. Goldstein killed your mother is because she went to see him shortly before she died?"

"That's not all. When we found her dead, I saw this little spot of dried blood on her arm, but I was so...I don't know...I just felt numb and couldn't think straight."

"You were probably in shock."

"I didn't think anything about it at the time. Didn't even mention it to the police when they said Mom had died of natural causes. So someone from the funeral parlor came and took her body. Then my husband made me a cup of tea and talked me into going to bed."

"It was good you were able to get some rest."

"The next day my best friend came over to help with the phone calls and I told her everything. When I got to the part where I noticed the dried blood, I suddenly remembered seeing a spot just like that after the nurse gave her a shot. I was sure she didn't have any blood on her when I washed her up just before we left and she couldn't have scratched herself, so that meant somebody had to have come in the house and given her a shot while we were gone. Since Dr. Goldstein was the only person who knew how much she wanted to die, it had to be him."

"What did you do?"

"I called one of the detectives who'd been out to the house and told her the doctor had killed my mother. She said she'd have the M.E. go to the funeral home and take a blood sample. I guess they can do that even though the body's already embalmed. The detective said they'd have the blood tested for toxins but it'd be a few weeks before they could tell us anything."

"I've heard the lab's really backed up."

A gust of wind blew strands of blond hair into Gwen's fleshy face. "It doesn't matter. The important thing is, when they analyze the blood they'll find poison in it and then I'll have my proof."

Proof that somebody killed her mother, but not proof the doctor did it. Especially if his alibi holds up.

Cassidy rummaged inside her purse, pulling out a notepad, pen, and business card. She handed the card to Gwen. "Would you mind giving me a call when the test results come back?"

"Um, I guess I could do that."

"And I'd appreciate it if you'd give me your number too so we can keep in touch." *Just in case she drops your card along with the cigarette butt in the nearest trash can.*

Gwen rattled off a number.

Cassidy dropped her pen and pad back in her purse, then reached out and ran her hand down the sleeve of Gwen's coat. "I'm so sorry about your mother."

Chapter 17

Zach was leaning against the counter chatting with the woman in the blue shirt when Cassidy went back inside. As she crossed to stand beside him, she heard him ask, "So, what does a med tech do?"

"Just about everything." The woman's bright red lips stretched into a grin. "The nurse and doctors would be lost without me."

For a moment Cassidy thought the med tech was a teenager. She had a slender frame, the top half clad in a shirt that cleaved to her skin like glaze on a doughnut. Loose strands of reddish burgundy hair fell across her eyes, while the rest of it was caught up in two stubby pigtails. Cassidy's gaze moved to the med tech's face, where she noted crinkly little lines radiating from the corners of her eyes and mouth. *Dresses like a teeny bopper but been legal to buy beer for at least a decade.*

"Hi, I'm Cassidy," she said, inserting herself into the conversation. "This must've been a tough day for everybody here."

The med tech nodded, her face turning somber. "Thank goodness Dr. Leavitt was supposed to be on vacation and didn't have any patients today. I locked myself in the bathroom three times and had a good cry. And I know it's been even worse for Jill and doctor. At least we've got until Monday before we have to start telling her patients."

"I don't envy you that job," Cassidy said.

"Dr. Goldstein is the one who'll be stuck doing it. The only bad part for me will be seeing how upset they are. Her patients are likely to take it really hard."

The man who'd been reading the newspaper came into the reception area and stood at the other end of the counter.

"Excuse me." The med tech went to take care of him.

Shortly after the man left, Dr. Paul Goldstein came through the doorway again. Stepping forward, Zach introduced himself and Cassidy. "I appreciate your staying late to see us."

"I don't expect I'll have anything to add to what Jill already told you, but let's go talk in my office." He led them to a room at the end of a corridor. Bookshelves lined one wall and framed certificates hung behind a polished wood desk. Cassidy and Zach took the small upholstered chairs in front of the desk while Goldstein lowered himself into a swivel chair behind it.

The doctor was in his mid-forties. Brown hair fringed a bald spot on top of his head. His face appeared sensitive. Sharp cheekbones, sunken hollows beneath them, a long thin nose and taut jawline.

Cassidy said, "I'm sorry for your loss, Dr. Goldstein." *Wonder how many times you're going to say that before this day's over.*

"Please call me Paul. I regret that you had to witness that scene in the waiting room. Sometimes people get a little off-balance when a loved one dies unexpectedly."

Zach asked, "What can you tell us about the vacation Claudia was supposed to be on?"

Paul reiterated the story they'd already heard. Zach asked a few more questions, getting the same answers as before.

Cassidy propped her elbows on the armrests. "When was the last time you saw her?"

"She was still here last Friday when I left. Finishing things up before her trip." Paul ran a hand over his bald spot. "There's something else. But if I tell you, it has to be off the record."

"No problem."

"She called me while I was driving home. A pharmacist had just contacted her about a prescription for Vicodin because he couldn't read the dosage. Turns out Claudia never heard of the patient, which means somebody got their hands on her prescription pad. Both of us have been guilty of sometimes leaving pads out in the exam rooms, so she called to warn me to be more careful. Said she was going to call Jill and tell her the same thing."

"Can you give me the name of the pharmacist?"

Paul frowned. "What does the pharmacist have to do with writing a tribute to Claudia?"

"I've got at least two stories to write. One will be a feature on Claudia and all the good work she's done. The second will be about the murder itself. And if the case doesn't get closed soon, I'll be doing some investigating."

The doctor narrowed his eyes at Zach. "You agreed to keep this off the record."

"Okay, no more questions about the pharmacist or the stolen pad."

Cassidy shifted in her chair. "Do you know of anyone who might've wanted to hurt Claudia?"

Paul's tan face went a shade lighter. "Claudia was so...she was just so likeable and good-hearted. I can't imagine why anyone would kill her." He gazed into space, looking as if he were running possibilities through his mind. "Well, there was...." He stopped and shook his head. "No, there wasn't anybody."

"Let's go off the record again."

"I shouldn't have said anything."

"But you did."

Paul scratched his nose with his index finger. "About four years ago a new patient—a woman—made an appointment with Claudia for a physical. We always have people fill out a medical history form on their first visit, and one of the questions is, 'Are you allergic to any medications.' A few months later, this woman came in with a strep throat. Before doctors administer any medication, they're supposed to ask the question again, but Claudia was exhausted and forgot to look at the form or ask about allergies. She gave the woman an injection of penicillin, and the patient died of anaphylactic shock right here in the office. Claudia was devastated."

Cassidy wondered what it would be like to make a fatal error with a client. *So bad you'd have to quit doing therapy and go wait tables. But Claudia obviously had more grit than you. She didn't let it stop her.*

The doctor picked up his story again. "The woman's husband went a little crazy. One time he tailgated Claudia all the way home and then, when she got out of her car, he pushed his face into hers and called her every name in the book."

Cassidy said, "She must've been scared to death."

"She wasn't, but she should've been. She had this sense of invulnerability." Paul ran his hand over his head again. "Maybe she'd still be alive if she hadn't been so damned fearless."

Zach said, "I presume he sued."

Paul nodded. "The lawyers settled a while back. The husband walked away with a pile of money and Claudia got stuck with a huge hike in her malpractice insurance. But she didn't complain.

Said it was only right, considering what she'd done."

"Did the husband make any threats?" Zach asked. "Did he stalk her or call her on the phone or anything?"

"There was only that one incident. Everything went through the lawyers so there was no reason for Claudia to have any contact with him."

"But when Cass asked if you knew of anyone who might've wanted to hurt her, the husband came to mind."

"A few years ago he probably did want to hurt her. But in all this time she hasn't heard a word from him. It doesn't make sense he'd suddenly come out of the woodwork and put a bullet in her."

"What's his name?" Zach asked.

"Can't remember. Claudia always referred to him as the husband."

Zach slipped his notepad into his pocket. "Well, that's about it. Thanks for taking the time."

They all got to their feet.

"There's one more thing," Paul said. "I want you to know I never blamed Claudia for the woman's death. The fault is in this insane system we've got where doctors are expected to work around the clock, then make life or death decisions. This kind of thing could happen to any of us."

Chapter 18

Zach pulled the Subaru away from the curb and waited for a break in traffic. Once they were underway, Cassidy said, "Interesting how Paul turned ambivalent on us a couple of times. First when he brought up the prescription pad, then later when he started to tell us about the angry husband. Both incidents reflect badly on the clinic, but he obviously wanted us to know."

"Happens to me a lot." Zach braked for a jaywalker who had dashed out in front of the car. "People can't resist showing off how much they know. They tell me stuff they should never tell a reporter, and not all of them are smart enough to go off the record. Then they're outraged when I quote them in my story."

"I run into something similar. When clients have a secret they're ashamed of—maybe something they've never told anybody—they reach a point in therapy where some part of them knows the secret has to come out. But there's always an opposite part that absolutely wants to keep it buried. So they get all conflicted and start dropping hints. Since I'm not a mind reader, I don't always pick up on them, but if they stay in therapy long enough, it all eventually comes out."

"How do you know it does?"

"What?"

"How do you know they tell you everything?"

She stared out the side window. "I guess I don't." *Hubris. You just want to believe you're so good your clients wouldn't be able to hold anything back.*

She turned toward Zach. "Are you dropping a hint yourself? Do you still have secrets you haven't told me?"

"I have this deep dark secret that I sneak food to Starshine behind your back."

"Hah! I can always tell because you leave a dirty spoon on the counter."

Cassidy's attention was briefly captured by an ancient Volkswagon bus in the oncoming lane. Psychedelic colors in a tie-dye design covered the body of the bus, with *Jesus* painted in curlicue script on the side.

After the Volkswagon passed, Zach asked, "Find out anything from that nutso woman who confronted Goldstein?"

"I did indeed." Cassidy recounted everything the woman had told her. Pausing at the end of her story, she added, "I'm inclined to think Gwen Dickert may be right."

"Sounds like a flake to me. Her case against the doctor is entirely circumstantial."

"If they find toxins in the mother's blood, it won't be."

"Anything's possible. But if it does turn out the mother was poisoned, I'd look at Gwen's husband. He probably got sick of taking care of a quadriplegic mother-in-law and hired a hit."

Cassidy shook her head. "My money's on Paul. You know what makes me think he did it? His alibi. An alibi that stretches over the entire time Gwen's mother was alone in the house. How common do you think it is to be surrounded by friends and family from noon to midnight?"

"A solid alibi is usually taken to mean the person is innocent."

"But how solid is it? Don't you think the doctor could have gotten somebody to lie for him?"

"His wife or mother, maybe. Most law-abiding citizens are reluctant to lie to the police."

"I still think his twelve-hour alibi is too much of a coincidence." Cassidy mulled over the possibility that Paul Goldstein had committed euthanasia. "We were just discussing how often people say things they shouldn't. Maybe Paul killed Gwen's mother, then let it slip to Claudia, and she threatened to turn him in. That certainly would be motive for murder."

"Except the timing's off. Claudia was seen leaving for her trip Saturday morning. Gwen's mother died sometime after noon that same day. Then Claudia was murdered Tuesday evening. Even if Paul told Claudia what he was planning to do before she left, it seems strange she'd take off on her trip without notifying the police. And your euthanasia theory still leaves us without a clue as to why she returned early."

You twist your brain into a pretzel trying to connect dots that don't connect, then Zach blows your hypothesis away with simple logic.

Cassidy's stomach began making its needs known. "Where do you want to go for dinner?"

He looked at the clock on the dashboard. Six-fifty. "Shit. I'm afraid you're going to have to eat without me. I'm down to the wire on my deadline. I have to send in five inches on the murder before eight. Libby was generous to give me as much time as she did."

Zach drove around the block because of the cul-de-sac at Briar and Austin Boulevard. Briar, the street their garage emptied onto, ran along the north side of their house. As they tooled past their dining room window, Cassidy saw a large orange cat stroll diagonally across Briar and disappear into the alley behind their garage.

She leaned forward. "That's the monster cat. The one I couldn't get rid of last night."

"Too bad. I was hoping he was on his way to somewhere else." Zach dropped Cassidy off at the gate and continued on to the garage.

Clambering up the steps to the concrete stoop, she fished around in the bottom of her purse for her keys. *Good thing you shut Starshine in the basement this morning.* She pushed the door inward and the calico came streaking out.

Chapter 19

Cassidy crossed her arms over her chest and watched as Zach came through the gate and walked toward the stoop. "Why didn't you tell me you let Starshine out of the basement?" she demanded.

"Why should I? I perform doorman services for Starshine all the time and don't tell you. You didn't say anything about keeping her in the basement."

"I assumed she was still locked up and didn't pay attention when I opened the door," Cassidy said in an accusatory tone. "And we just saw the orange cat go into the alley."

Zach gazed at the calico, who was delicately nibbling grass in the middle of the yard. "Yeah, I see the problem."

"We've never been able to catch her when she's outside, and there's no way I'm going to leave her out here with that tom lurking around." Cassidy pushed a strand of cinnamon hair behind one ear. "I guess I'll just have to sit on the porch and wait till she comes to me."

"I'd do it but I have that story to write."

"Stay where you are while I get a warmer coat." Dashing inside, Cassidy changed into a heavy jacket, then returned and sat on the bottom step. She knew that eventually the calico would come over to get some petting.

Zach stood on the stoop looking down at her. "Whatever you do, don't get in the middle of a cat fight. I saw a woman in the ER once who'd tried to rescue her cat and she had deep cuts all over her arms and legs."

"Okay," Cassidy said, knowing she'd do whatever it took to protect Starshine.

"You're not listening." Zach went inside and brought out a straw broom, which he laid on the steps next to Cassidy. "You can beat the tom cat off with this."

"Go write your story. We'll be fine."

She knew the sun was slipping below the horizon in the west, but from where she sat on the east side of the house, the pale blue sky seemed to rise into infinity, with an iridescent light reflecting off a few puffy clouds. On the ground the light was slowly fading.

Cassidy's eyes roved from one side of the yard to the other, searching for the orange tom. The large rectangular yard was enclosed by a chain link fence with two entry points, a gate leading to the sidewalk and a gate leading to the alley. A lilac tree, surrounded by a patch of tall weeds, grew in the corner near the alley gate. A torn Doritos bag was caught in the section of fence that marked the southern edge of her property. Junipers clustered between the fence and the stoop.

She forgot her rumbly stomach and took delight in watching Starshine pounce on invisible bugs. From time to time, Cassidy scanned the fence that marked the perimeter of her yard. She was looking in the general direction of the lilac tree when she glimpsed movement out of the corner of her eye. The orange cat had flattened itself to the ground and was squeezing beneath the alley gate. She stood and grabbed the broom, but before she could take a single step, the cat disappeared again.

In those tall weeds back there. Given the ease with which cats could slink from one hiding place to the next, she didn't think bashing the weeds with her broom would do any good.

Starshine was only a few feet away, stalking something Cassidy couldn't see. *Close enough you*

could beat the monster off if he tried to attack her.
But even though she kept telling herself the calico
wasn't in any real danger, she could feel pressure
building in her chest.

She scrutinized the weeds and bushes growing
along the south section of the fence. At its closest
point, the fence was only about eight feet from the
stoop. As the light turned dusky, it became
increasingly difficult for her gaze to penetrate the
tangled growth. She glanced at Starshine, sniffing
the grass not far from where she sat.

Looking toward the fence again, she saw a pair
of round yellow eyes peering out from the stand of
juniper bushes growing near the stoop. The eyes
were fixed on Starshine. Cassidy's first impulse
was to bring the broom down on the cat's head. *No,
don't! The second you stand up, the cat will be gone.
And Starshine will be freaked as well.*

She remembered that on some rare occasions,
the calico had been known to come when called.
Especially if she'd had her fill of being outside.

"Here, kitty, kitty," Cassidy crooned.

Starshine looked at her as if considering her
request.

"Here, kitty, kitty. C'mon over here."

The calico meandered toward the bottom step.
She rubbed the side of her face against Cassidy's
shoe.

*Take a deep breath. Move slowly. If you try to
grab her, she'll run.*

Cassidy took a quick look at where the yellow
eyes had been. The monster cat had left the
junipers and was running toward Starshine, who
hadn't seen him yet.

Grabbing a handful of scruff, Cassidy scooped
the calico into her arms. She jumped to her feet,
sending the broom clattering to the ground. She

flew up the steps and gripped the doorknob. As she was opening the door, she felt a claw dig into her left calf. Gasping for air, she crossed the threshold and closed the door behind her. Starshine wriggled free and raced out of sight.

Cassidy took a moment to get her breathing under control, then sat in one of the waiting room chairs and propped her left ankle on her other knee to inspect the damage. The tom's claw had ripped a hole in her best black pants and left a deep bloody gash in her flesh. A slight tremor ran down her legs as she stood and peered through the window in the door. The orange tom sat on the porch staring up at her.

Now I understand why people associate cats with the devil.

Cassidy doused her wound with antiseptic, then stood in front of the kitchen window and devoured a handful of peanut butter cups. She made three tuna fish sandwiches, carrying two up to Zach and eating the third in the dining room by herself.

She went up to the bedroom and tossed her low-heeled pumps onto the closet floor with a sigh of relief. Her feet were much happier in the grubby gym shoes she wore around the house. She put them on, then took her notebook out of her purse and plunked into her desk chair. Swiveling toward a darkened window, she propped her feet on the radiator cover beneath it.

St. Claudia...surrogate mom...dedicated to her patients...beloved by all who knew her. This woman is way too good to be true. So what's her dark side?

People are reluctant to speak ill, etc. But I seem to recall that some of her friends hinted at imperfections.

Cassidy turned back toward her desk and opened her notepad. After reading what Jill had said about Claudia's relationship with her mother, she jiggled a pen between her fingers and mulled it over.

Is an inability to forgive an imperfection? Or is it just the way human beings are made?

According to therapeutic dogma, everyone would be better off if they could forgive the people who'd hurt them. Many of her clients worked on achieving forgiveness and most had made progress. But even her most successful clients acknowledged that the old anger still popped up from time to time.

You can see it in yourself. On some rare occasions you even get pissed at your ex all over again.

In your experience, total forgiveness seems to run against the grain of human nature.

Chapter 20

She went back to reading her notes. A comment made by the neighbor Madison regarding Claudia's "bad habit of falling in love" caught her attention. At the time Cassidy assumed that the "bad habit" was a pattern of picking abusive men like Jordan, but now she realized there were other possible interpretations. *And the person who would know what Madison meant is Jill.*

Cassidy found Jill's home number in her notes and picked up the phone.

"I've come up with a few more questions," she said to the nurse. "Do you have time to talk?"

"Just a minute." A short pause. "I was watching a movie. I rented five on the way home. Whenever I'm in a funk, I load up on movies and sweets. I've already finished off a bag of chocolate chip cookies."

Cassidy noticed that Jill's voice was much flatter now than when they'd talked earlier. *Delayed reaction. Claudia's death just now sinking in.*

"If you don't feel like talking, we can always put this off for another time."

"No, don't hang up. When I was at work, I couldn't wait to get home so I could be alone. But now...I was so glad to hear a friendly voice on the other end of the line."

"I felt like that after my divorce. Wherever I was, I wanted to be someplace else. Nothing was right."

"So, what's on your mind?"

Hearing cat paws clumping up the stairs, Cassidy turned to face the doorway. "One of the people we talked to said Claudia had a bad habit of falling in love and I'm not sure what she meant by that."

Jill breathed raggedly into the phone for several seconds. While Cassidy waited for the nurse to respond, Starshine sauntered across the bedroom and sprang onto her desk.

"I'm such a terrible person. My best friend was just killed and here I'm feeling an urge to gossip about her."

"Of course you want to talk about her. You want me to know what kind of person she was. That's how we always feel when we lose someone we love."

Starshine rolled onto her side, stretching to her full length and completely covering the pad Cassidy intended to take notes on. She scratched the cat's neck.

Jill said, "So you think it's okay for me to tell you about this weird thing she had going on with men? She went through boyfriends faster than I go through M&Ms. Sometimes I thought she was part witch, the way she could cast a spell over any good-looking guy who came within ten feet of her. Not when she had her doctor's hat on, you understand. She never messed with patients. Only in her personal life. Sometimes we'd go out together and I'd watch her do it. She'd see some guy that interested her, they'd strike up a conversation, and boom—they'd both be instantly in love. That never happens to me. Claudia is...was pretty, but she usually wasn't the hottest chick in the room. I guess it must've been pheromones or something."

"I've heard about women like that." *Usually from the men who get snared by them.*

"So anyway, Claudia would meet some guy, they'd both fall head over heels, she'd carry on this intense relationship for a while, and then all of a sudden it'd be over. It was like a switch went off inside her. She'd simply lose interest and walk away. Of course the guy never knew what happened. He'd be calling night and day. I always felt sorry for the men when she was done with them."

Wasn't like that with Jordan. He drove her away.

"What was Claudia's attitude about it? Was she cavalier? Did she feel guilty?" Cassidy slipped her fingers underneath Starshine's white stomach and tried to pull her notepad out without disturbing her. The calico sat up, shot Cassidy an indignant look, and stalked off.

"She didn't know why her feelings turned off the way they did," Jill answered. "You know that old song—'the feeling's gone and I just can't get it back?' She told me she felt bad about it—but not really bad, you know what I mean? Not bad enough that she wouldn't turn around and do it again."

"How long did she go between these—what would you call them?—crushes?"

Jill snorted. "She thought of them as great love affairs. No, she didn't really. She'd make jokes about herself and say she ought to be in therapy."

She was right about that.

"But how long was it between—"

"Anywhere from a couple of weeks to three or four months. Never long enough for her to get sick of sleeping alone. Me, I'm lucky if I meet someone I like every year or so."

Cassidy had worked with enough single women in their thirties to know that quality men in that demographic were in short supply. "So what you're saying is, she wasn't very selective."

"On paper they all sounded great. She wouldn't have anything to do with guys unless they were smart, and she especially went for creative types."

"Any chance she also went for bad boy types?"

"Not that I could tell. There was this one creep she took out an order of protection against, but according to her, all the others were alternate versions of Mr. Wonderful. My guess, they could've been jerks and she wouldn't have noticed." Jill took in a breath, then let it out slowly. "Jeeze, what kind of friend am I, bad-mouthing her right after she was murdered?"

"I wouldn't call it bad-mouthing. You're just filling in the gaps, making her into a real person."

"I don't know what's wrong with me. I can never keep from running off my mouth."

"But you're helping me out. So, did Claudia have any theories about why she kept falling in and out of love?" Cassidy picked up the loose pens on her desk one by one and stuck them in a floral-patterned mug.

"Oh, she threw around a lot of buzz words. Talked about fear of intimacy and love addiction. Me, I think she did it for the adrenaline rush. Who wouldn't want to live half their life in a state of euphoria?"

Cassidy laughed. "Sounds exhausting. I doubt I'd be up to it." *Infatuations are great, but over the long haul I'd rather have a nice steady supply of love and comfort.*

"Exhausting or not, I wouldn't mind giving it a try."

"I've never had that kind of male attention in my life," Cassidy replied. "Wasn't it hard on you to see your best friend reeling in boatloads of men?"

Jill took a moment to answer. "I can't say the green-eyed monster never came to call. But most of the time I felt sorry for her. I expect to get married and have kids someday. Claudia's life didn't seem headed in that direction."

"Not from what you tell me. Before we talked, I didn't have a sense of her. She seemed too perfect, not like anyone I've ever met. Now I feel like I know who she was."

"Is there anything else I can help you with?" Jill sounded as if she didn't want the conversation to end.

Cassidy fished around in her head for another question. "You said Claudia was still in the office when you left last Friday. Did you get a call from her later?"

"No. Why would I?" Jill's voice took on a guarded tone.

"Dr. Goldstein said she called him about a stolen prescription pad and that she was planning to call you next."

"Half the time I run around with a dead battery in my cell. Lot of good it does to have a cell phone if you can't remember to put it on the charger."

"Well, that's all I can think of for now," Cassidy said. "Maybe you can call somebody else. Talking usually helps."

"You planning to send me a bill?" Jill snorted again. "I'll be all right. I've got my movies and snacks."

Chapter 21

Cassidy hung up the phone, her thoughts drifting to Jordan. She wanted to know what happened to him. *Good chance the cops picked him up and he's still at Area One.* This was the name of the detective unit that served the near south side of the city.

Still, wouldn't hurt to leave a message. That way, you might hear from him when he gets home. If he gets home. If he's willing to talk to you.

She pulled her Rolodex to the front of her desk and searched through the dog-eared cards for Jordan's number. *Be easier to find people if the cards were in exact alphabetical order instead of approximate. And if you threw out the cards for people whose names have long since slipped out of your memory banks.*

She found her former client's number and called him. When his voicemail came on, she left a message urging him to get back to her.

At eight-fifteen Zach came into the bedroom. He raised his burly arms in a long stretch, then sank into his desk chair.

Cassidy swiveled to face him. "Did you find out anything about Jordan?"

"All I know is they haven't arrested him. The press liaison did her 'no comment' routine, which means nobody's been charged."

"But with that order of protection, the cops must be looking at him as a serious suspect. Since it hasn't been forty-eight hours yet, they're probably still holding him."

"Depends. Jordan would've had a few hours between the time he left here and the time the cops knocked on his door. If he pulled himself together, disposed of the bloody shirt, and didn't admit anything, all the cops would have is an expired order—not nearly enough to build a case. That is, not unless the cops found the murder weapon in his house."

"I still think there's a good chance he didn't do it. Especially now that we know about Claudia's mysterious trip, which doesn't seem to have anything to do with Jordan."

"Yeah, it seems like her vacation—if it even was a vacation—must have some connection to her murder."

"So what's next?"

"After I filed my story, I looked up the husband of the patient who died of anaphylactic shock. Considering it's been a few years since it happened and the suit's already settled, it seems unlikely he'd suddenly decide to pop Claudia. But he's the only person we know of other than Jordan who had a reason to dislike her, so I figure it's worth talking to him."

"What did you find out about him?"

"Works in sales for a telecommunications company. Owns a home in Evanston. Has a couple of kids. No criminal record. I'm going to set up an interview for tomorrow."

Zach called on the cordless and Cassidy listened in on her desk phone.

"Is this Ray Franklin?"

An affable voice on the other end confirmed that it was.

"This is Zach Moran from the *Post*. Did you know that Dr. Claudia Leavitt was murdered last night?"

"I heard about it on the drive in to work," Franklin said. "Man, was I surprised. I almost rear-ended the car in front of me."

"I was told that Dr. Leavitt caused your wife's death."

"That was three years ago. I only saw the doctor once. After that the lawyers handled everything."

"I'd still like to talk to you. What time tomorrow could you fit me in?" Zach dug around in the papers on his desk and pulled out his cell phone.

"Look, I understand you've got a job to do, but it'd be a waste of both our times. I don't know anything about the doctor."

"I'll keep it short."

"If I say no, I suppose you'll hound my nanny and rake through my trash."

"When people say no, it makes me wonder what they've got to hide."

"You've got it all wrong, man. I just don't like to talk about Randi's death. For three years now, I've been trying to put it behind me."

"I realize this may be difficult, but I need to interview you before I can wrap up my story. Give me a time and place. Oh, and I'll be bringing my wife. She's researching a book."

"My kids count on me to come straight home from work so we'll have to do it at my house. Say five-thirty. You got my address?"

"Yeah. See you tomorrow." Zach disconnected.

"I feel sorry for him." Cassidy picked cat hairs off her black pants, which had already been ruined by the orange tom. "We're going to stir up painful memories. I would've been tempted to let him off."

"Yeah, but you wouldn't have done it."

Pig-headed.   That's what your mother used to say.   Once you decide to do something, you don't let anything stop you.

Mror! Starshine said in a loud angry voice. She stood on her hind legs and extended her front paws to rattle the back doorknob.

If cats had opposable thumbs, they'd be the master race.   Cassidy chugged some coffee and waited for her brain cells to blink on. *Why am I not opening the door?   Oh, I remember.   There's a devil cat out there waiting to maul and maim her.   This monster made such a big impression on Zach that even he—the soft touch in the family—refused to let her out.*

Cassidy had awakened a few minutes earlier in a bed that was missing a husband.   When she straggled downstairs, she found a note from Zach next to the coffeemaker. She filled her mug, added cream and sugar, then read the note:

I went in early to knock off my assignments so Libby won't object when I take time off to pursue the investigation. Love, Zach

Starshine said *Mror* again, a banshee sound impossible to ignore.

Oh shit! What are you going to do? If you let her have the run of the house, she's likely to sneak out when your clients open the door this afternoon. But you don't really want her to live in the basement. Best bet would be to shut her in the bedroom so she can sleep on the waterbed and be close to you.

Cassidy moved toward the howling cat who had plastered her body against the door.   As Cassidy reached down to grab her, she ran between her human's legs, raced across the kitchen, and disappeared through the dining room doorway. Cassidy sprinted after her.

She stopped in the living room, where Starshine often sought refuge behind either the sofa or the loveseat, which faced each other on opposite sides of the room. Cassidy looked behind the sofa first, where the cat wasn't, and then behind the loveseat, where she was. Chasing down the calico was a familiar game, and Cassidy knew all the moves.

She went to one end of the loveseat, the end from which she could see Starshine's head, and shoved the piece of furniture out into the middle of the room. Then she got down on all fours and crawled toward the cat, who somehow managed to turn around in the narrow space and scoot out the end that was still against the wall.

The calico scrambled across the room to hide behind the sofa. Cassidy grunted as she put her shoulder to the heavier piece of furniture and pushed it away from the wall. Once again, Starshine escaped and this time she raced up the stairs. Trailing behind her, Cassidy smiled. She knew where the cat was going, and it was exactly where she wanted her to be.

Cassidy went into the bedroom, closed the door, got down on her hands and knees again, and peered behind the waterbed. Starshine gazed smugly back at her.

"Pleased with yourself, aren't you? You know this is the one place where nobody can get you. But guess what? I'm going to keep the door shut"—*at least as long as I can hold the thought*—"and force you to be an inside cat, which is what you should have been all along. And I don't give a rat's ass how you feel about it."

You can't leave her in here without a litter box. A cat box in the bedroom? Yuck.

Cassidy carried the box from the landing in the basement stairs up to the bedroom, closed the door behind her, and got into the shower.

Chapter 22

A little after eleven the phone rang. Cassidy stopped cleaning the bathroom mirror and picked up at her desk.

"It's me." Her grandmother's sprightly voice sounded on the other end. "I wanted to let you know I referred a client to you about a week ago. Granddaughter of a friend of mine."

"Hey, thanks. I can always use more clients." *Except when you're in the throes of an investigation. But half the people who get referred never follow up.*

"So anyway, I called to see if Becky'd made an appointment. 'Course I know you can't tell me either way, but I figured it gave me an excuse to ring you up."

Cassidy drew a cheerful cartoon face with big hair on the back of an unopened envelope. "You don't need an excuse. You can call me anytime."

"In my day people didn't phone just to chat. You had to have a reason, and even then you kept it short. 'Course I know the whole world's different now. Everywhere you go, people are talking on cells and a lot of folks have little plastic jobbies growing outta their ears. They even talk on the phone when they take a pee."

"I can't bring myself to do that. I'm always afraid the person on the other end will hear the water splash."

"So how's it going?" Gran asked. "You keeping yourself busy?"

You should tell Gran about Claudia's murder. You know there's nothing she likes better than a good mystery, and a lot of times she comes up with something you haven't thought of.

"I'm glad you called. Zach and I are full throttle on a new investigation."

"And you're gonna tell me all about it?"

"You have any plans for lunch?" Cassidy asked.

"Am I having it with you?"

"I'll pick you up at noon and we'll go to Erik's."

Gran stepped out onto the wide wooden porch extending across the front of her stucco two-story. A three-inch high silvery gray wig wreathed her small gnarly face.

"I've never seen you with gray hair before," Cassidy said.

"I got this friend, she's not even half my age, and she let her hair go gray. It looked so good on her, I decided to give it a try." Gran fluffed her stylish wig. "What do you think?"

"It's very handsome but I have to admit my all time favorite is the Brenda Starr one."

"I'll wear it next time. That is, if I'm in a Brenda Starr state of mind I will. I always go with what fits my mood."

They climbed into Cassidy's elderly Toyota and drove to Oak Park's restaurant row, which began on Lake Street and extended south along Oak Park Avenue. Within a four-block radius, diners could choose among Indian, Greek, South American, Mexican, Asian, Italian, Middle Eastern, and American cuisine.

Bypassing the cuisines, they headed toward their favorite deli. After placing their orders, they picked a table and sat in aluminum chairs with black vinyl seats. The remodeled deli was a large room with an industrial look to it. Large geometric blocks in avocado and burnt orange added interest and warmth.

Gran unwrapped the napkin containing her silverware. "Now let's get to it. I can't wait a minute longer."

Cassidy leaned toward Gran and lowered her voice, then began telling her everything that had happened since Jordan rang their doorbell Tuesday night. She was interrupted by a busboy delivering their plates, a quesadilla for Cassidy and an Erik Burger for Gran. She waited until he was gone, then finished her story.

Gran removed the top half of her bun and nibbled on the tiny french fried onions piled on her hamburger patty. "You and Zach sure did manage to collect a lot of information in just one day. So who have you got lined up as suspects?"

"As much as I hate to admit it, we can't rule out Jordan. The husband of the woman who died doesn't seem to have much of a motive after all this time. The one I really like is the mystery man."

"Maybe they went on a trip together but this Dr. Claudia couldn't tell anybody because he was hiding it from his wife. And while they were away, she got sick of him and told him to buzz off. So they went back to her house and he shot her."

Cassidy stared in awe at her grandmother. "That's brilliant. It ties everything together."

Gran sat tall, patted her wig, and preened.

"The only problem is," Cassidy continued, "we have no idea who he is or how to find him."

"Won't the dees be able to trace him through her emails and phone luds?"

"You learned that from watching cop shows, didn't you?"

Gran nodded.

"Well, you're right. The cops probably do know who he is. But if Jordan has Claudia's blood on his shirt and the mystery man doesn't, the cops are bound to be more interested in Jordan." Cassidy took a bite of her quesadilla and chewed in gloomy silence.

Gran worked away at her hamburger, then laid down the last section, wiped her fingers, and said, "Didn't you say the other person you couldn't find was the sister? Any chance she was involved, since there was bad blood between her and the vic?"

"Doesn't seem likely. According to Jill, Claudia and Hailey haven't had anything to do with each other for a long time. Hailey may not even know her sister's dead. Of course her mother might have told her. If her mother even knows how to reach her." Cassidy considered the various possibilities. "Oh shit! What if nobody told David?"

"Who's David?"

Cassidy explained the relationship between Claudia and her nephew. "It'd be terrible if David tried to reach her after her trip was supposed to be over and she didn't respond. And he had no idea why."

"That poor kid!" Gran balled one tiny hand into a fist and pounded it on the table. "If Claudia's mother hasn't told Hailey and David, we'll have to track him down and do it ourselves."

"Let me see if I can get hold of the mother."

She called Zach and he gave her Ellen's number. Ellen confirmed that she hadn't spoken to Hailey in years and didn't know where she was.

Cassidy dropped her cell into her purse. "I guess that means it's up to us." She rubbed her fingers back and forth along one side of her face. "Let's see, where do teenage boys hang? Oh, of course, on Facebook."

Gran gave her a wide grin. "Everybody's on Facebook. Everybody except you."

"I suppose that means you have a site."

"Page, not site. I keep hoping you'll show up. Then we could write on each other's walls."

"What's wrong with talking on the phone?"

"Nobody does that anymore."

"I suppose you're going to give up your landline and only communicate through Facebook, texting, and tweeting."

"I thought about it, but I like to gab too much."

Picking up the last slice of quesadilla from her plate, Cassidy demolished it, then wiped the grease off her hand with a napkin. "So—since you're the pro and I'm the novice—you're going to have to show me how to find David on Facebook."

"You wanna do it now? I was gonna visit a friend in the hospital, but I could put that off."

Cassidy looked at her watch. "I've got a client in an hour, but I don't have anything on my calendar for tomorrow morning. How 'bout ten o'clock at my place?"

"I'll pick up some chocolate donuts."

Chapter 23

Cassidy went into the bedroom to get ready for her client, reminding herself to shut the door behind her so Starshine couldn't get out. She picked up a book-sized engagement calendar from her desk. Everyone she knew recorded their appointments in their phones, but her Luddite propensities led her to stick with the old and familiar.

Close to midnight on Tuesday when Zach made his anonymous call. And now it's Thursday afternoon. Cassidy knew the police could keep suspects for up to forty-eight hours but they often didn't hold them that long.

She called Zach and asked him if he could find out whether the cops considered Jordan a suspect and if they did, whether they were still questioning him.

The phone rang twenty minutes later.

"They hauled him into the station, held him several hours, then released him."

"But they'll keep trying to build a case against him, won't they?"

"Maybe. But given that Claudia had a mystery man in her life and left a trail of broken hearts, the cops may well have a number of other suspects to look into by now."

Cassidy hoped Jordan would respond to the message she'd left on his voicemail.

Ray Franklin, the husband of the woman who died of anaphylactic shock, lived on a block of large homes set close together, most of them lacking any distinctive architectural features. As Zach searched for the address, Cassidy observed a couple of women chatting on the sidewalk, two small boys riding bikes in the street, a cluster of teenage girls shooting hoops in a driveway. *Lot like our block.*

Zach parked in front of a two-story frame house with a weathered wooden swing on its porch. The surrounding yards were in better shape than Franklin's, which had untrimmed bushes and clumps of matted leaves left over from the fall. Cassidy could sympathize. *Before Zach moved in with his yard-maintenance gene, your lawn contributed dandelion seeds to all the properties around you. And your neighbors frequently didn't respond when you said hello.*

Zach banged the brass knocker. A tall man with an athletic build, dark chocolate skin, and an amiable face opened the door. He wore blue suit pants, a pink open-throated shirt, and a loosened tie.

"You must be Zach Moran." He nodded at Cassidy. "And Mrs. Moran."

"Cassidy McCabe," she said, smelling alcohol on his breath. "I kept my own name."

"Come on in." Franklin stood back so they could walk past him into the foyer. His features were regular, with arched brows and thick curly lashes. A pencil mustache traveled in two thin lines from his upper lip to his jaw, then formed a fringe along the bottom of his chin.

Their host ushered them into a living room divided into two sections. In the front half, a teenaged girl and a younger boy sat in front of a TV playing a video game. In the back half, two sofas stood at right angles to each other, facing a square coffee table.

Franklin stood in front of the television screen and spoke to his children. "Man, I told you kids you'd have to go outside when my visitors came."

"Cammie's grounded," the girl whined. "There's nothing to do."

"Just get your asses out of here," Franklin said in a good-natured tone.

Moving as slowly as possible, the children took jackets out of the closet, stuck arms in sleeves, and left the house.

Their father, hands resting on hips as he watched them leave, shook his head. "They usually fight me when I tell them to come in. Only reason they were in the house today is they knew someone was coming and they wanted to eavesdrop."

He picked up a short glass from the coffee table filled with dark amber liquid. "Can I get you something?"

"No thanks," Cassidy said.

Zach shifted his weight, letting his body go loose. "I'll have what you're having. On the rocks."

Cassidy knew Zach believed that drinking along with sources put them at ease.

"Be back in a minute." Franklin walked toward the rear of the house. He returned shortly and handed Zach a glass.

Cassidy and Zach sat on one sofa, Franklin on the other. He took a swallow of his drink, then placed his glass on the wooden table. From the number of rings already there, Cassidy could tell this was not a family that believed in coasters.

"I looked up your story online," Franklin said. "The murder sounded pretty gruesome. I shouldn't have read it, man. I don't need those pictures in my head."

Chapter 24

"She died instantly," Zach said. "Didn't suffer at all."

"Yeah, but having some lunatic in her house forcing her to undress...." Franklin hunched forward, a tremor passing through a muscle in his cheek. "Must've been pretty terrifying."

"You seem upset by her death," Cassidy observed.

"Not really." Franklin ran his fingers through his short beard. He paused a moment before continuing. "Well, I guess I am a little. I had trouble sleeping last night. I kept reliving the whole thing...I mean, what happened to Randi. I did that for quite a while after she...then it finally stopped. But last night it all came back."

"What an awful time. For you and the kids."

He gulped half his drink, then set the glass down and stared into it. "The other thing is, I was sorry to hear what happened to Dr. Leavitt. For a long time after I lost Randi, I was so pissed at the doctor I couldn't see straight. Then I started talking to someone and realized it really was just a horrible mistake. Tragic for us, but tragic for her too."

"I give you a lot of credit," Cassidy said. "Most people can't muster much empathy for someone who's caused them so much heartache."

Sounds like this is someone who can forgive.

"Thanks." Franklin lifted his glass, then set it down again. He looked at Zach. "Do the cops think the killer is someone she was involved with?"

"They're not talking. But from the description of the crime scene, I'd say it was either a lover or an ex."

"After you called, I started wondering if the police are going to question me."

"I'm surprised you haven't heard from them already. You must be near the bottom of their suspect list. But if you haven't seen Dr. Leavitt in all this time, you won't have anything to worry about."

"Have you seen her?" Cassidy wanted to know.

"No, man, why would I?"

"Do you have an alibi?" Zach asked.

Franklin's head snapped up straight. He glared at Zach. "I just told you I haven't seen her."

Cassidy picked up a Spiderman action figure from the table and set it on its feet. Choosing her words carefully, she said, "I understand there was an incident...that the two of you had words." *Actually, he did all the talking.*

"Christ!" Franklin ran a hand over his face. "You're not going to put that in your story, are you? It's the most embarrassing thing I've ever done."

"What exactly did you do?"

"I waited for her to leave the clinic, then rode her bumper all the way to her house. When she got out of her car, I said some things I regret." He paused. "You have to understand, I was beside myself with grief. I've never done anything like it before or since."

Zach took a sip of his drink. "When was the last time you saw her?"

"That was. I made sure I stayed away from her after that." He rubbed his knuckles through the hair on his chin.

Cassidy tilted her head to one side. "The sudden death of your wife...I imagine your life must have changed dramatically after that."

Franklin took in a long breath and let it out slowly. "Used to be I was pretty ambitious. Had a good job, pulled down six figures. But I spent half my time traveling. After Randi was gone, the kids needed me here, not flying around the country. So I took a demotion. Man, did I resent it at first. Ben was acting out all over the place and Sara hardly spoke to me. Then I found a child psychologist who helped me deal with the kids and we eventually settled in. Not that everything's wonderful. I'm constantly pulled in ten directions at once, and no matter how hard I try, the kids never get as much attention as they need. But for now we're doing okay."

"I assume you got a decent settlement," Zach said, "so at least you can afford good professional help."

Franklin's mouth pulled down at the corners. "It pays for the nanny and the psychologist. But most of it went into a college fund."

As they descended the sagging wooden steps, Cassidy noticed the temperature had dropped several degrees while they'd been inside. Feeling a chill creep into her bones, she zipped her jacket all the way up, then clutched her arms across her chest. *April weather—more unpredictable than a celebrity under the influence.*

Glancing up, she could see neither clouds nor sky, merely a gradual shift of light from dull white near the ground to deep charcoal at the uppermost reaches of her sight.

They got in the Subaru and Zach hung a U-turn, cruising back the way they had come. "I had the sense Franklin was telling the truth when he said he wasn't pissed at Claudia any more. So if he wasn't carrying a grudge, there goes our motive."

"He did seem frustrated about having to give up his big bucks salary, but there wasn't the least hint he blamed Claudia for it."

"I'm sure he felt cheated on his settlement. People always do. You know—I lost my wife and all I got was this lousy hundred grand. But if he blamed anybody for that, it'd be his lawyer."

The traffic light turned green and the SUV in front of them didn't move. Zach tapped lightly on the horn and it started into the intersection.

Cassidy said, "The only time I felt a little twinge was when he reacted so strongly to Claudia's death. But after he explained it, it seemed to make sense."

"Okay, so we cross Franklin off our list. We didn't think he was a likely candidate anyway." Zach reached over and squeezed Cassidy's knee. "Now we need to think about us. We're right in the middle of rush hour and there's no good way to get from Evanston to Oak Park. Let's look for a decent restaurant and hope the traffic's lightened up by the time we finish dinner."

Chapter 25

Midmorning and Cassidy was putting on the second pot of coffee for the day when the back doorbell chimed, announcing her grandmother's arrival. She went around the room divider into her reception area, where Gran's wiry figure was hanging a black leather jacket on one of the hooks by the door. Burnished red curls tumbled around the octogenarian's narrow shoulders.

"You wore the Brenda Starr wig. Is that because I said it was my favorite? Or because you were in a Brenda Starr mood?"

"A little of both. Can't you just see the sparkles dancing 'round my eyes?" Gran was referring to the little crosses that appeared near the eyes of the Brenda Starr comic strip character.

Cassidy peered into her grandmother's wrinkled face. "Why yes. Now that you mention it, I can."

Gran handed Cassidy a Dunkin' Donuts bag, and Cassidy arranged six chocolate donuts on a plate. She poured coffee, put everything on a tray, and carried it upstairs to the computer room, with Gran close on her heels.

"Here, will you hold this a minute?" Cassidy transferred the tray to Gran, cleared off some space on the computer table, and set the tray down. "You need to sit in front of the monitor and show me how this Facebook thing works."

Plunking herself down in Zach's chair, Gran lowered the seat several inches so she could plant her feet on the floor. Cassidy settled in her own chair and rolled it close to her grandmother's.

Gran logged on and pulled up Facebook. "What do you wanna do first? Search for that boy's profile? Or take a peek at mine?"

You really want to look for David.   But Gran's dying to show off her handiwork.

"Let's see yours."

Gran typed in "Lola."

"Lola? Who's she?"

Lola's profile appeared on the screen.   Her picture displayed a voluptuous young woman with enormous breasts nearly falling out of her flowing cream-colored dress.   Golden curls crowned her seductive face. Lola's friends were all male.

"Wow!" Cassidy said.   "Where'd you get that picture?"

"Off the Net."

"You're such a whiz.   I could never just pluck some picture off the Net."

"Sure you could.   You just aren't interested enough to spend hours learning how to do it."

"Well, you're right about that."

In Lola's "About Me" section a series of short blog entries marched down the page. Cassidy read the last one. "My philosophy of life: Be nice and have fun."

"Somehow I get the impression that Lola's not exactly nice."

Gran cackled. "Well, I hope not! She's my alter ego. She does all the things I could never do. She may not be nice but she sure does have fun."

"Let's look for David Leavitt," Cassidy said. She held her breath as Gran typed his name into the search box and hit enter.   Another box appeared indicating that there were one hundred and eighty-three David Leavitts on Facebook. Gran refined the search by location and narrowed the number down to one.

A photo of a teenager appeared on the Chicago David Leavitt's page.   It revealed a short-haired, clean-cut, muscular boy pouring some kind of liquid from a test tube into a beaker. A caption below the picture said: Mad Scientist. Beneath the caption was a box with a few lines of small print.

"Here's hoping this is Claudia's nephew," Cassidy said.

"'Course it's blocked. But that shouldn't matter since all you want to do is message him."

"I've heard that all the kids use privacy settings to keep adults out."

"Not just the kids. Almost everybody uses them. But I don't need 'em 'cause Lola wants everybody to see everything."

Cassidy read aloud the lines of print inside the box. "I wanna become the strongest dude on the planet. I wanna win a Nobel Prize in science. I wanna star in a martial arts film. I wanna have the biggest dick in school."

"How could he tell if he had the biggest dick?" Gran asked.

"I don't know. Maybe they hold contests."

Gran swiveled to face Cassidy. "It's kinda odd that he put so much information on his profile. Most kids don't tell you anything 'cept maybe their school or sex." Gran nibbled on the tip of one stubby finger. "But then some kids like to put things up just to be different."

Cassidy waved her donut in the air. "I didn't even know how to get on Facebook and here you've found David in less than a minute."

Gran, who adored praise, bestowed an incandescent smile on Cassidy. "I suppose you want to message him now."

"Right."

"We still got one little problem. Since we're using my account, the message will look like it's coming from Lola."

"Oh." Cassidy twisted her garnet ring. "Well, I'll just have to make the best of it. Let's switch chairs so I can use the keyboard."

Once she was settled in Gran's chair, she clicked on the message link. She began by filling in the subject line: "Info regarding your Aunt Claudia." Then she composed her message. "I'm not Lola. Lola let me use her account to find you. Jill told me about your relationship with your aunt and I thought someone should contact you. I know it must seem weird that a complete stranger is emailing you about Claudia, but I'll explain when I see you. Please get back to me as soon as you can." Cassidy signed her first name, followed by her email address.

"What do you think?" she asked her grandmother. "Will it make him suspicious? Will he read sexual predator between the lines?"

"He won't know what to make of it, but he'll be so worried about his aunt he'll have to answer." Gran cocked her head at Cassidy. "Why'd you only use your first name?"

"So he can't Google me. God only knows what might be out there about my lurid crime-solving past."

Cassidy clicked *send*.

"You'll have to let me know as soon as you hear from him." Gran started to pick up the tray but Cassidy took it out of her hands. They went downstairs and finished off the donuts.

Cassidy couldn't concentrate. She tried to plan dinner but the knot in her stomach made it impossible to think about food. She wandered around the house looking for Starshine and was reassured to find the calico sleeping beneath the hanging clothes in her closet. She killed half an hour with an overdue call to her mother, which gave her an opportunity to practice her listening skills.

A voice in her head kept rehearsing what she would say to David. She looked at the bedroom clock. *Only one-thirty. He won't get out of school till after three. But maybe he checks his email on a school computer.*

She logged on and skimmed the subject lines of her incoming mail. The last one was the line she had written. The sender was madscntst.

"What's wrong with Claudia? Why R U messaging me instead of Jill?"

Jill? She said she didn't have any way to contact him. But he must think she does.

Cassidy hit reply. "I'm sorry to make you wait, but this is something I have to tell you in person. You pick a time and place and I'll be there."

She wondered if David was currently online and whether he might IM her. She'd never received an instant message before but felt sure she'd recognize it if it appeared on her screen. A few minutes passed and nothing happened so she went outside and rode her battered old bike around the neighborhood. The sky was gray and dark clouds were blowing in from the west. By the time she returned to her house, drops had started to fall.

The next time she signed on, a second message from David awaited her. "WHAT'S WRONG WITH CLAUDIA? TELL ME NOW!"

She repeated: "Pick a time and place and I'll be there."

Half an hour later, David acceded to her demand. He gave her his cell number and the address of a McDonald's in Hyde Park and said he'd meet her there at four o'clock.

Chapter 26

When she parked in the McDonald's lot, a steady drizzle was coming down and the light had turned smoky. She entered the half-filled restaurant and scanned the customers. A teenager who matched the photos on David's website sat rigidly erect at a table near the rear of the room. As she approached, he stood and shot her an angry look.

"She's dead, isn't she?"

The careful sentences Cassidy had rehearsed were useless now. There was nothing she could do but nod.

He bolted for the men's room.

For a moment Cassidy stood rooted to the floor. She realized she was breathing in shallow gasps so she went to the counter intending to get coffee. *Just what you need—caffeine to amp up your adrenaline level.* She asked for a paper cup and filled it with water instead, then sat watching the men's room door. A short time later David came out and exited the McDonald's without even glancing her way.

What's he doing? He can't just leave. Nobody could walk away without getting all the details. Unless he Googled her and read the news reports. But then he wouldn't have had any reason to meet you.

Cassidy looked out the window and saw him in the parking lot standing in the rain. David lit a cigarette. Hunching his shoulders, he cupped his hand over the burning end. His short hair was a lighter shade of blond than Claudia's. He wore baggy jeans and a tee shirt imprinted with the Grateful Dead insignia. His shoulders and arms

were so bulked up they looked out of proportion to
the rest of his body. He ambled around the parking
lot, lighting a second cigarette off the first.

He threw the cigarette on the ground, then
came inside, water dripping from his hair, his tee
shirt plastered to his muscular chest. Moving in
slow motion, he drifted over and sat across from
Cassidy. His pupils were dilated and the acrid
smell of pot hovered around him.

She asked, "Did you Google any of the news
about your aunt's death?"

"No."

*Didn't want to find out any sooner than he had
to.*

Cassidy moistened her upper lip. "Someone
shot her inside her house. It happened Tuesday
night."

"Burglary?"

"The police think it was someone she knew."

"One of those dudes she kept jumping in bed
with?" His voice was mellow, with no hint of
judgment or blame. "What's your connection? Why
are you telling me instead of the cops?"

"My husband is a crime reporter for the *Post*.
He's investigating Claudia's murder."

David shook his head. "I still don't get it. What
does that have to do with you?"

"I'm working with Zach on the investigation. I
felt you should be notified but nobody knew how to
reach you. Then someone suggested Facebook."

David frowned. "Jill's got my email address.
She should have messaged me right away."

"She told me she didn't know how to get in
touch with you."

"Bullshit. I heard from her just a few weeks
ago."

She lied to us? Because she didn't want us to talk to David or Hailey?

"Do you know of any reason Jill would try to keep us from finding you?"

"She wouldn't do that."

Maybe you misunderstood what Jill said. Looking down at the table, Cassidy moved her paper cup in slow circles. "How's your mother doing?"

"Hailey? She's pretty much stoned all the time. But she's not my real mother. She never lifted a finger to do anything for me. But that's okay. I like it that she doesn't pay attention. That way I get to do whatever I want."

Cassidy heard loud voices yelling jocularly back and forth. She looked toward the door to see a gang of teens that had just come pushing and shoving into the restaurant. She was glad they took two tables on the opposite side of the room.

She turned toward David. "Your mother doesn't take care of you so you have to do everything for yourself?"

He leaned back and gave her a mocking smile. "Hey, I'm fifteen. I don't need anybody to take care of me. Besides, I've got Claudia." His face went blank, the coloring draining away. "I mean, I used to have Claudia."

"What did she do for you?"

"She started me on Karate and weight lifting soon as she found out Hailey was going for custody. After I moved in with her and her dickhead boyfriend, they forced me to go to the local school, even though Claudia offered to pay for a private school. That Stone Park school really sucks. Some of the bangers tried to hassle me, but I knew enough Karate by then to fight them off. Now nobody bothers me."

"What about Hailey's boyfriend? Does he ever bother you?"

"He tried beating on me right in front of her and she didn't say a word. But I was able to flip him and then he left me alone."

"Does he ever beat on Hailey?"

"The weird thing is, he acts like he's crazy about her. He's this really tough, really mean dude, but he gets all soft and mushy around her."

"Is there anything else Claudia did for you?"

How bad will it be that she's not there any more?

"Oh yeah." David shook a cigarette out of a pack of Camels and put it between his lips but didn't light it. "She set up a bank account and gave me a debit card so I'd have my own money. She kinda cheered me up when I was down and cracked the whip when I got off track. She was always on my case to keep up my grades so I could get into a good college."

Really bad!

"Living with Hailey and her boyfriend sounds pretty awful but I get the impression you're doing okay. Is that true? Or is it just because you're high right now that you seem to be coping?"

David took the cigarette out of his mouth and put it back in its pack. "Being high helps. But I don't do it very often. Claudia's constantly warning me that I could end up like Hailey. When I first moved in with her and the dickhead, I was so fucking pissed I wanted to kill someone. Then Claudia and I figured out what to do. The trick is to stay away from the apartment. So I spend most of my time hanging with my friends from Hyde Park. I take an el and two buses to get from here to that shitty Stone Park school, then after school I come back to Hyde Park. My buds all let me sleep at their houses so I almost never have to go home.

Hailey doesn't notice and her boyfriend's happy to have me out of the way."

Cassidy heard a burst of laughter. She turned to see a large teenaged male in a tee shirt that hung down to his knees swaggering toward them.

"Yo, freak," he said to David. "I need them smokes."

David stood, his shoulders squared, his arms bowed out slightly from his sides. The other boy was taller, but he looked soft and paunchy next to David.

Madscntst took a step forward. "Go get your own smokes, shithead."

The belligerent teen looked at him for a second, then waved a hand downward. "Naw, that's not my brand." He turned and strode slowly back toward his friends, who were laughing and jeering.

Cassidy said, "I guess you *don't* have to worry about being hassled."

David sat down again. "We done yet?"

"I just have a couple more questions. I'm curious why Claudia didn't report Hailey when she started using again."

"I never told her."

"Why not?"

"Hailey hates Claudia for taking me away. She hates her like you wouldn't believe, even though she doesn't give a shit about me. And the dickhead is one scary dude. I was afraid he might go after Claudia if she tried to get me back. Then, after I worked it out so I didn't have to go home more than once or twice a week, I decided I like my life the way it is."

"I suppose you like it because you don't have to be accountable to anybody."

He smiled a slow hazy smile.

Cassidy pulled her pad out of her purse. "Would you mind giving me your official address?"

"You wanna talk to Hailey? It won't do you any good. She hasn't had any contact with Claudia since they sat on opposite sides of a courtroom waiting for a judge to decide where I was going to land."

"Any reason you wouldn't want me to talk to her?"

"Naw, I don't care. I won't be there anyway." He gave Cassidy his address.

Sticking a cigarette between his lips again, he lit it and stood. "Gotta go. Karate class in half an hour."

Chapter 27

Cassidy drove north through the increasing traffic, her hands clutching the steering wheel as she struggled to see through the smear of rain on her windshield. Her heart ached for David. The woman he thought of as his real mother was dead. His birth mother was too drugged out to care where he spent his nights. His grandmother showed no interest in him, and he probably didn't know who his father was. Claudia was all he'd ever had.

When kids were faced with overwhelming loss and had no one to walk them through it, their lives often came apart. They numbed out on drugs. They turned rageful and violent. They sank into depression. They killed themselves.

Chances are David's headed for serious trouble.

The car in front of her braked suddenly and Cassidy was so preoccupied she nearly rear ended it.

David's situation reminded her of her stepson, who'd lost his mother at the age of seventeen. When Bryce's mother discovered that her life was in danger, she sent her son to Zach for safekeeping, even though she'd never told him that their brief fling had resulted in the birth of a child. To Cassidy's and Zach's shock, Bryce appeared at their door one day and announced that Zach was his father.

For a long time after his mother's death, Bryce had been sullen, hostile, and depressed, but Cassidy and Zach were always there to watch over him. Now in college, he seemed to be doing well.

Cassidy needed to turn left at the next intersection but found herself stuck in the right lane. *Stop dwelling on the past and attend to your driving.*

When she arrived home, she went upstairs, sat at her desk, and played the message Zach had left on their voicemail.

"I'm working late tonight. Don't go confronting any killers without me. See you around nine."

She reached for the phone.

Don't be silly. Just because you were thinking about Bryce doesn't mean you have to call him. In fact, he usually sounds annoyed when you do.

It's not being silly. Stepmoms are supposed to annoy their kids by calling to show they care.

After eight rings, Bryce answered in a groggy voice.

"Did I wake you? If you're sleeping, I can call back later."

"Yes, you woke me. And no, I'm not sleeping. I had to get up to answer the phone."

"I'm sorry. Your schedule is so erratic I never know when to call."

"You should let me be the one to call. Then you'd never run the risk of calling at an inopportune moment. Like, for instance, if I had a girl here."

"If I had to wait for you to pick up the phone, I'd never hear from you. What's wrong with my wanting to stay in touch?"

"Look, I'm a college student. You might as well face it. Nothing you or Zach does is ever gonna be right."

"Okay, I understand. This is a time of life when you need to push us away."

"Would you drop that patronizing tone. I hate it when you *understand* everything."

She smiled to herself. *If Bryce is so determined to give you a hard time, it's good to be able to give a little of it back.*

"So," he said, "what was it you felt you had to tell me this time? That I need to get enough sleep or my brain won't develop properly? That I should get straight A's but shouldn't study too hard? That I should always use condoms when I have sex?"

"I don't say things like—"

"Yes you do. First you tell me to have fun and make the most of my college years, then you tell me not to drink or drug too much. Like there's any other way to have fun. The only thing anybody around here ever does is party, and that means—"

"I know what it means. I just don't want you to overdo it."

"So how much is too much? Is it okay if I pass out drunk one night a week but not three? How often would you find it acceptable for me to smoke dope or do X?"

Cassidy's curiosity was almost limitless. As a therapist, she was used to exploring every aspect of human behavior. But Bryce's questions reminded her that there needed to be a boundary between parents and their almost adult kids.

"Okay, I give. I don't want to know how much you're doing of anything."

"Don't worry. I tend to be the designated driver."

"I'll try not to give out any more motherly advice. I hardly ever do it with clients but I can't keep my mouth shut with you or Zach."

"That's all right. Don't tell anybody, but I really don't mind you harassing me. It gives me something to complain about when everybody else is bitching about their parents."

Cassidy hung up feeling pleased. Bryce had initially rebuffed her, just as he was supposed to, but he was still clearly engaged enough to want to spar with her.

She was sitting on the bed reading a book when the phone rang. She picked up the cordless from her nightstand.

"This is Jill. I found something I thought you might be interested in."

"What?"

"Claudia's purse. I knew right away I should tell the police, but nosy me, I had to bring it home where it'd be easier to snoop through without anybody finding out I had it. That Nazi part of me that makes me do the right thing seems to have gone missing."

Somehow "Nazi" and "right thing" don't seem to belong in the same sentence.

Cassidy brushed a loose strand of hair back from her face. "If I found Claudia's purse, I would've wanted to see what was in it too."

"You don't think it was so bad that I took it home?"

I do think it was bad but I'm glad she did.

"I don't see any harm. You can always report it to the police tomorrow. So what did you find?"

"A picture of Claudia snuggled up next to this guy I've never seen before. No name or date. Maybe it's her mystery man. Anyway, I thought you might want to take a look before I turn the purse over to the cops."

Chapter 28

"Now there's an offer I can't resist." Cassidy shifted, trying to adjust the pillows behind her back. "I could drive to your place right now."

"I'm leaving to meet some friends in a few. Could you come to the clinic tomorrow morning? If you park in the lot behind the building, I could slip out the back and sit in your car to show you the picture. That way Doctor and Kelly won't know that I'm meeting you. I don't want them finding out I discovered the purse and didn't say anything."

"Sure, I can do that. But I don't understand how she could have left her purse at the clinic. Didn't she have her keys in it?"

"She kept one of those small dressy purses in her desk, and whenever she went out after work, she changed from her old battered one to her dressy one. I remember about a month ago she was complaining that she couldn't find her regular purse."

"Where was it?"

"Way back in the corner of the coat closet behind some junk. I was cleaning out the closet when I stumbled across it. Amazing how things turn up in the strangest places. Even the police missed it when they came to haul out her stuff."

Cassidy asked, "What time should I meet you?"

"Can you make it at ten?"

"No problem." *You should ask about the email she sent David. But how can you do it without sounding accusatory? Last thing you want is to lose her friendship.*

"So how did it go today?" Cassidy queried.

"Doctor's keeping Claudia's door closed. She usually left it at least partway open so we could pop in if we needed to.   Every time I see that closed door...."

"It's a constant reminder.   There must be so many of them."

Cassidy heard Zach's footsteps on the stairs and swiveled toward the bedroom doorway.   He came into the room, the mail Cassidy had left on the porch in his hand.

"Did you finish everything on your list?" she asked.

"I'm all caught up for now, so Libby shouldn't have any problem with my taking time off for the investigation."   He sat at his desk to sort the mail.

Considering you've got more free time than he does, you shouldn't always leave the mail for him. You just conveniently forget it because it's such a pain.

Turning toward her, Zach dropped some envelopes on her desk.   "Looks like five new charities have you in their scope."

"I talked to Claudia's nephew today.   And Jill has a picture to show me."

"So Gran's idea of looking on Facebook worked."

Nodding, Cassidy told him of David's reaction to hearing about the murder.   While she was talking, Starshine came trotting into the room and sprang onto Zach's lap.   The calico emitted a loud rumbly purr and lifted her face for chin scratching.

"Looks like you didn't have any more catly dramas," he said, interrupting Cassidy's story.

"Starshine started to give me a hard time about not letting her out, but then she fell asleep and forgot about it.   And I didn't see any sign of the orange tom."

"That cat's bound to move on sooner or later."

"You didn't let me finish." Cassidy went on to tell him about Hailey's drug habit, her boyfriend, and the ways David had learned to cope. "I feel so sorry for him. Here he is, basically a good kid, and his life was already a mess. Now—without Claudia to provide encouragement and money—it's bound to get a whole lot worse."

"Why don't you report Hailey?"

"David's set up his life so it's stable and he gets to spend most of his time with his friends. If Hailey lost custody, he'd get dumped into the foster care system, which, as we all know—"

"Is for shit."

Starshine curled into a ball and gave Cassidy a smug look as if to say, "I picked him over you."

"Anyway," Cassidy said, "David gave me his home address so now we can pay Hailey and her boyfriend a visit."

Zach stroked the cat's back. "If Hailey hasn't seen her sister in years, she won't be able to tell us anything and she definitely wouldn't qualify as a suspect."

"David said they haven't seen each other, but how would he know?" Cassidy rubbed her fingers against the arm of her chair. "Don't dopers tend to get a little paranoid?"

"They can."

"David stressed how much Hailey hated Claudia for taking him away. So maybe Hailey assumed David and Claudia were emailing each other and convinced herself that Claudia was going to try to regain custody. Which she undoubtedly would have if David had told her about his mother's drugging. If Hailey thought Claudia was out to get David again, she might have sicced her really mean, really scary boyfriend on her sister."

Starshine jumped down. Zach leaned back and laced his fingers behind his neck. "That's not half bad. It doesn't fit my enraged lover scenario, but it would give Hailey a motive. Okay, I agree, we need to talk to her. Now what about this picture Jill wants to show you?"

"She found a purse Claudia lost about a month ago. She didn't tell Paul Goldstein or the med tech because she wanted to sneak it out of the office, take it home, and look through it."

"Sounds like something I'd do." As a reporter, Zach had conducted more than his share of unauthorized searches.

Cassidy told him about the man in the photo and her plan to meet Jill behind the clinic the next morning.

"Jill's certainly going out of her way to be helpful. Doesn't it strike you as a bit odd that she'd want to show you the picture?"

"Not really. I think she's feeling guilty about not reporting it to the police and she had the sense I'd be supportive. You know, those nonjudgmental vibes I give off."

"I wish you'd send more of them my way."

"You're my husband. It's my job to keep you in line."

"So what are the odds you'll recognize this dude in the picture?"

She tightened her lips and looked away, not wanting to acknowledge the point he was making. Letting out a breath, she answered, "Next to nothing."

"So why spend an hour in city traffic going to look at the face of someone you've never seen before?"

"You know the answer to that. Because I'm just like you—too obsessive to let any stone go unturned."

"When you finish wasting your time in Edgewater, give me a call and I'll pick you up at the house so we can drop in on Hailey."

Chapter 29

Cassidy turned into the lot behind the clinic and parked next to a gleaming red two-seater convertible. Two cars sat on the other side of the sports job, a black SUV and a beige hatchback, both looking dowdy in comparison.

Figures. Flashy convertible for the doc, sedate inexpensive cars for the nurse and med tech. Paul Goldstein didn't strike you as the flashy type, but who knows what fantasies of hot cars and hot women lurk inside the breasts of the most mild mannered of men.

She wondered if Zach harbored such fantasies. *Naw. If he was attracted to hot women, he wouldn't have married you, and if he lusted after a sports car, there'd be one inhabiting your garage now. Besides, Zach isn't exactly your Walter Mitty type.*

Cassidy, mostly indifferent to cars, studied the convertible, thinking it looked familiar. *How could that be? You never pay attention to what anybody drives.*

Then she remembered. One of her wealthier clients had insisted on showing off his new Porsche. She'd let him drag her out on the stoop to get a better look at it. Her client's car was white, but other than that, it seemed quite similar to the one she was sitting next to now. *So the convertible's probably a Porsche. Not that it matters. The brand of car the doctor drives has absolutely nothing to do with his proclivity for murder.*

Five minutes until ten. Cassidy opened her window and picked up an unpleasant odor. Near the clinic's rear entrance sat a dumpster with a shopping cart half filled with debris standing at an angle next to it. As Cassidy was wondering where the cart's owner had gone, the head and shoulders of a man in an oversized suit coat popped up out of the dumpster and tossed a handful of cans into the cart, raising a loud metallic clatter.

Before long, Jill came through the door carrying an envelope. She climbed into the Toyota's passenger seat and said, "This worked out just like I hoped. Doctor's with a patient and Kelly's at the counter, so nobody saw me leave."

Cassidy twisted sideways to face Jill. "This is totally irrelevant, but I'm curious about that red convertible. Is it a Porsche?"

"Yep. Dreamy, isn't it?

"It's sweet, all right, but I can't see myself driving it. I'm more of a Toyota kind of girl. Although I could go for red."

"You wouldn't want to drive a Porsche?" Jill's green eyes filled with pity.

Too tame for a sports car? You are pathetic.

Cassidy hastened to change the subject. "So, let's see the photo."

Jill handed her the envelope.

Cassidy stared at a picture of Claudia with her blond head nestled against the shoulder of a man with coffee-colored skin. She managed to stop herself from saying "Omigod!" but couldn't hold back a sharp intake of breath.

Jill's eyebrows shot up. "You know who he is."

"Um..." Thoughts darted through Cassidy's head as she searched for a way to deny that she'd seen the man's face before. "I thought I recognized him," she said weakly, "but now that I look more closely—"

"You think I'm stupid? Well, maybe I am. I opened up completely to you and now you're trying to lie to me about knowing who that man is. Even though I'm the one who found the picture and offered to show it to you."

She's right. You're being unfair. And there's no real reason you shouldn't tell her.

"I'm sorry. It was just an automatic reaction. When Zach's running an investigation, he never tells anybody anything and I just sort of picked it up from him. You were very generous to let me see this picture and I shouldn't have tried to keep anything from you."

"So c'mon, dish. Tell me who he is."

"The last person either of us would've expected to see with Claudia. Remember the woman who died of anaphylactic shock? And the husband who tailgated Claudia all the way home?"

"I can't believe it. You mean Claudia's mystery man is the husband of the woman she killed? No, wait, I didn't mean 'killed.' I just meant...well, you know." Jill twisted one of her many gold rings.

"That's who this guy is." Cassidy touched her fingernail to the man's face. "Ray Franklin. We talked to him a couple of days ago. But since there's no date on the picture, we can't be certain he's the mystery man."

"Sure we can. Ray Franklin was the only one she didn't talk about. Every other dude, she used his name, told me what kind of work he did, rhapsodized over his wonderfulness. But not with Ray. She said she'd met somebody new and he was sweet and sensitive and intelligent—she had long strings of adjectives for all of 'em—and that she couldn't say anything more because he wanted to keep their relationship a secret. I just assumed he was married."

"Had she dated married men before?"

Jill hesitated. "I couldn't say for sure."

She could, but she's not going to. So *Jill isn't totally open after all.*

"Can I borrow the picture for a day or so? Zach and I are going to need to confront Franklin with it. He told us he hadn't seen Claudia since the tailgating incident."

Jill's head reared back. "You think he killed her?"

Cassidy held the picture in front of Jill. "This certainly moves him up on the suspect list, although we can't assume he's guilty just because he lied. He had a pretty obvious reason for not wanting anybody to know he was involved with Claudia. So, can I take the picture?"

A tiny vertical line appeared on Jill's forehead. "I should give it to the police."

"The police are way ahead of us on Franklin. I'd be surprised if they haven't grilled him already."

"But how would they know?"

"By looking at Claudia's phone calls and emails."

"So it doesn't really matter if I give them the picture or not?"

"You should give it to them because it's the right thing to do, but it doesn't matter when."

"All right, you can borrow it, but I want it back when you're done. I'll feel better once I hand the purse and everything in it over to the police."

Cassidy wriggled out from behind the steering wheel and stretched toward Jill to give her a hug. "This is a huge help. I can't thank you enough."

Chapter 30

Cassidy was on her hands and knees wiping mud off the waiting room floor when Zach opened the back door.

"Is Starshine inside?" he asked as she got to her feet.

"Why? Did you see the monster cat?"

"He was in those bushes next to the garage. I nearly had to kick him to get him to leave."

"It's a good thing you didn't. He might've chewed your foot off." The wound the tom had inflicted on Cassidy's calf had scabbed over but she still felt a twinge when she twisted it the wrong way.

"What about Starshine?"

Cassidy wrinkled her forehead, trying to remember if she'd seen the calico since returning from the clinic. "She didn't get past me when I was coming and going so she must be in the house."

They found her curled up in a fuzzy cat bed on the computer table. Cassidy's mouth eased into a smile. Just watching Starshine sleep gave her a sense of well being.

Zach laid his hand on Cassidy's shoulder. "You ready to pay Hailey a visit?"

"Let me get my purse and jacket."

Cassidy settled into the Subaru's passenger seat, then turned toward her husband. "Remember last night when you were making fun of me for driving all the way to Edgewater to look at the picture Jill found?"

"I wasn't making fun of you."

"You were so sure I wouldn't recognize the man Claudia was with."

"But evidently you did, so tell me who it was."

"I think I'd rather gloat first."

"Go ahead. Gloat as much as you want."

"It was Ray Franklin."

"Now that's interesting."

"I love it when you're wrong."

Zach traveled west to Mannheim Road, turned north, and drove through Stone Park, the suburb where Hailey lived with her boyfriend. Cassidy gazed at a string of sleazy taverns, interspersed with massage parlors, gentlemen's clubs, and small dilapidated houses. Zach made a couple of turns, then pulled up in front of a low-rise apartment building that was a cut above the others they'd seen in Stone Park. No garage littered the small strip of lawn. The wooden door was clean. The buttons for the intercom system were intact and clearly labeled.

Cassidy skimmed the names. "Oh shit. No 'Hailey Leavitt.' I should have gotten the boyfriend's name."

Zach punched the top button. No one answered. He punched the second button. A heavily accented Hispanic voice wanted to know who was ringing his doorbell.

"I'm looking for Hailey Leavitt."

"Try Earl Grapski."

Zach pushed the Grapski button.

A woman's voice issued from the intercom. "Come on in. I'm on the second floor." A buzz sounded and they went into the hallway.

Cassidy's brows drew together. "She didn't even ask who we are."

"We got lucky. It might've been tricky to talk our way in through the metal grate."

They climbed a flight of stairs. Halfway down the corridor, a slender young woman stood near an open door waiting for them. As they moved closer, Cassidy appraised the woman's appearance. She wore a white tee with a wispy pink kitten on the front and rhinestone-studded jeans that managed to look expensive rather than tacky. Her pale blond shoulder-length hair curled under at the ends, and her sky blue eyes sparkled.

Cassidy couldn't stop staring. *You were expecting cadaverous, jittery, bags under the eyes. This woman doesn't look anything like the junkies you've seen on TV.* Since Cassidy had no addictions training, she'd never been exposed to people who were serious users.

Hailey cocked her head and asked in a chirpy, sing-song voice, "Are you Jehovah's Witnesses? I had two nice young men talk to me about religion just a few months ago."

Zach rested his hands on his belt. "There's something we have to tell you. About your sister. But first we need to go inside and sit down."

"Yes, let's do that." Hailey went into her apartment and Cassidy and Zack trooped in after her.

Doesn't know who we are. Didn't react to the mention of her sister. I'm starting to feel like we've fallen down the rabbit hole.

Hailey waved expansively toward a royal blue sofa and two canary yellow chairs. "Make yourselves comfortable while I go get us something to drink. Is tea okay? I always like a nice cup of tea in the afternoon."

Tea and cocaine—or crack or heroin. What more could you want?

"Tea will be fine," Zach said.

Hailey whisked off into the kitchen.

Zach grabbed a handful of bright pink and yellow pillows from one end of the sofa, dumped them on the floor, and sat down. Cassidy piled identical pillows in the corner of the sofa's other end and parked herself next to Zach. An entertainment center holding a huge flat screen TV stood against the opposite wall. A rectangular coffee table, its surface littered with takeout cartons and beer cans, stood in front of the sofa.

Hailey brought in three cups on a tray. She handed one each to Cassidy and Zach, then pulled a yellow chair closer to the table, sat down, and claimed the third cup for herself. Noting the absence of a sugar bowl, Cassidy set hers on the table.

It's not like she's going to notice whether I drink her tea or not.

Hailey swished the teabag in her cup. "I don't think you told me who you are yet."

"Zach Moran. I'm a reporter for the *Post*. And this is my wife, Cassidy."

"A reporter! How exciting!" She flashed a bright enthusiastic smile.

"I'm afraid I have bad news." Zach paused. Hailey's smile didn't waiver. "Your sister Claudia was murdered in her home Tuesday night."

Cassidy couldn't detect the slightest change in Hailey's expression. *It's as if Zach delivered a weather report instead of a death notification. Is that because she knew already? Or because she's too stoned to care?*

"So, are you gonna interview me?"

"When was the last time you saw your sister?" Cassidy inquired of the rhinestone-studded woman.

"Oh, I don't know." Hailey swiped at the air dismissively. "Claudia was mad at me. She resented that David chose me over her."

Cassidy forced herself to maintain a neutral expression and not to let her jaw drop.

"When did David choose you?"

"A few years ago. He could see that I was a much better mother. She was always working. Didn't make time for him. All she cared about was money. But I was satisfied to stay home and raise my son. Now that David's living with us—"

Hailey was interrupted by the creak of the front door opening. They all turned to look at the thickset man who came through it. His scalp was shaved, his upper lip adorned by a lush black handlebar mustache. He had a round head, short neck, and broad muscular shoulders. He was clearly strong, but no match for Hailey's weight-lifting son.

"Hey, babe!" Jumping up, Hailey ran over to give him a hug. "We've got visitors. This is Zach Moran. He's a reporter and he's going to write a story about me for the *Post*."

Earl looked straight at Zach. Wrapping an arm around Hailey, he turned her body toward the sofa so Cassidy and Zach could watch as he fondled her breast, his fingers squeezing her nipple. Cassidy felt as if the air were growing thick.

Chapter 31

He dropped his hand, turned his back on them, and strode into one of the other rooms.

"He's not very talkative," Hailey explained, returning to her chair.

Zach scratched his jaw. "Getting back to what you were telling us, it sounds like David was living with Claudia before he moved back in with you."

"He did for a while, but it was all a mistake." Hailey stuck a strand of hair in her mouth and chewed on it. "Well, not a mistake exactly. It was Claudia being mean because I had what she wanted."

"How was Claudia mean?" Zach probed.

Hailey's carefree smile faded. "She took David away from me when he was just a baby. I needed him so much. I needed him to love me. The only time in my life I was unhappy was after she took him."

I bet she found something to swallow, snort, or inject that got her to soaring again.

"You said Claudia took him because you had what she wanted," Cassidy observed.

Hailey's pretty face turned radiant again. "I had a child and a boyfriend who took care of me. All Claudia ever had was her work. She was jealous of me, even when we were kids. After Dad died, Claudia had to cook and clean and do everything Mom used to do, but I could just go out and have fun. I always had lots of boyfriends and Claudia didn't even date."

Claudia missed out on dating when she was young so now she wants to rack up as many conquests as possible? Naw, nothing's ever that simple.

"So," Zach said, "how did she manage to get custody?"

Hailey's expression darkened. "She lied about me to DCFS. She had friends there. She pulled strings."

Cassidy picked up a fork from the table and laid it on a dirty plate. "What did she say about you?"

The younger woman looked away. "She said I was stoned when she came to visit. I admit I smoked weed now and then. I mean, who doesn't use something when they're stressed? Food, pills, whatever. But I wasn't hooked or anything. It was just recreational. I mean, DCFS never takes a baby away because the mother has a glass of wine in the evening."

Getting defensive. You better reel her back in. "That does seem pretty harsh. You must've been devastated when they gave David to Claudia."

"That's exactly how I felt."

"Is Earl David's father?"

"Oh no. I only stayed with his father a couple of years, then he disappeared on me. He was...let's see...what was his name?" Hailey paused to sip her tea. "When will your story be in the paper? I wouldn't want to miss it. I've never had anybody write a story about me before."

"Don't know yet. I've still got some loose ends to tie up." Zach stood. "You've been very helpful. Thanks for the time."

Cassidy and Zach cruised past a scantily dressed Latina standing on a street corner. Cassidy did a double take. "Is that what I think it is?"

"Yep."

"I thought they only came out at night."

"Street corner girls have to work whenever they can."

Cassidy briefly felt sorry for the woman, then her thoughts returned to the interview. "So what do you make of it that Hailey didn't react at all when you told her Claudia'd been murdered? Was it because she's high? Or because she knew already?"

"You mean, knew already as in killed her?"

Cassidy stared at a small sedan, its rear end crumpled as if a larger car had tried to mount it. "I didn't get the sense that Hailey had anything to do with killing her sister. You know the story she told about David choosing her over Claudia because she was the better mother? That's just the sort of rationalization people create in order to avoid facing the truth about themselves. I'm convinced she believes it, and that would put her one-up on Claudia. When people feel one-up, they seldom have a need to seek revenge."

"You want to take her off the suspect list?"

"Yeah, I do. Unless you think she wasn't surprised because her really mean, really lewd boyfriend did the deed."

"Naw, I don' think that's it. When people are as wasted as Hailey, nothing's likely to faze them. What you said sounds right. If she really believes David chose her, she isn't likely to feel threatened or vindictive."

"Well, you certainly know more about being wasted than I do."

"Was that a dig?"

"Um...I guess so."

"Where did that come from?"

"You used to get high like Hailey."

"And you're pissed about that now?"

"I know, it doesn't make sense."

"Yeah, I used to get high. I loved getting high. There's nothing like it, not even sex. But I held down a job and was more or less in touch with reality and I quit when I realized it was messing up my life."

"I know. I should've kept my mouth shut."

They drove several blocks in silence. Cassidy looked out at neon beer signs hanging in a series of darkened windows.

"You want to know something else?" he said. "When we were with Hailey, I started reminiscing about what it felt like to be stoned all the time and I had a brief fantasy of going back to the life. But I'd never do it because I have too much to lose. And the most important thing I have to lose is you."

A feeling of warmth uncoiled inside her.

She looked at Zach. "It was pretty weird, that display her boyfriend put on. You think it was exhibitionism? Or a demonstration of ownership?"

"I'd say it was his version of flipping us off."

Chapter 32

Cassidy and Zach sat in the Subaru in front of Ray Franklin's unkempt yard. The air felt like spring and a golden light flowed from the large orange ball hovering just above the western skyline. But the tension in her stomach prevented her from appreciating the first warm day of the season.

She looked at her watch. "It's five-thirty. Confrontation time."

"Let's give him five more minutes. Make sure he has a chance to loosen his tie and pour himself a drink. Or whatever it is he does when he first gets home."

Cassidy, who wanted to get it over with, frowned at her husband. "This isn't going to be fun."

Zach shrugged. "You can hang back and let me do the talking."

"You know I won't do that."

A minute later she pulled on the door handle. "This is long enough. I'm going to go talk to him."

She led Zach up the concrete walkway and onto the front porch. The door opened and Franklin stared at them in surprise.

Cassidy jumped in before Zach could take control. "Sorry to just show up like this, but some new information has come to light that contradicts what you said before."

She noted a flicker of fear in his brown eyes. Then his face hardened and his pupils became opaque.

"This isn't a good time." The door started to close.

Zach stepped forward. "You want to read a news story that ends with 'Franklin declined to comment?'"

He stood motionless for a couple of beats. "What story would that be?"

"This is too complicated to discuss on your porch," Cassidy said. "We need to go inside and sit down."

Franklin let them in.

After they were seated, Zach said, "You told us you hadn't seen Claudia since the night you followed her home."

"That's right, man. I haven't."

Cassidy took the photo out of its envelope and held it in front of him. His expression didn't change.

"What's that got to do with me?"

"It proves you had a relationship with Claudia," Cassidy said. "A relationship you went to some lengths to hide."

"I suppose you think that's me."

Cassidy turned the picture around so she could look at it. "I see a pencil mustache, with two lines of hair going from the corners of the mouth to the jaw, and a thin beard along the chin. I don't *think* it's you. I *know* it's you."

"Oh, so I'm the only black man who ever had a beard like that?" His lips curled in a sneer. "The problem is, you can't tell one black dude from another. We all look the same to *you people*."

Zach laughed. "Well, that's original. We have a photo showing you and Claudia together and you're just going to deny it's you."

"You write a story claiming I'm the guy in the picture and I'll sue your ass into the poorhouse."

"Good luck with that." Zach started toward the door and Cassidy followed.

Cassidy fumbled with her seatbelt, making several attempts before she succeeded in getting the buckle to snap into place. "Gran and I were bouncing ideas around, and she thought Claudia might've gone on vacation with her mystery man, which would've given her a reason to be secretive about it. But after they'd been together a few days, she got tired of him and blew him off. So then they came back to Chicago and he shot her."

Zach whistled under his breath. "They should clone Gran's brain."

"That theory would explain just about everything."

"She would've dropped Franklin off, then had to park in her garage without anybody seeing her. But that wouldn't be unusual because people generally don't notice much. He would've had a gun in his house and gone straight to her place and killed her."

"I suppose the police have already checked to see if he was at work Monday and Tuesday," Cassidy said.

"Yeah, they probably have. And we should find out too. But I won't be able to talk to anybody at his workplace until Monday."

"Even if he was in town, he still could have done it. Claudia could have decided it was over while she was on the road, then come back to tell him in person. And he could've gone berserk just like he did in the tailgating incident." Cassidy rested her chin on her fist. "So what do you think? Is Franklin a better suspect than Jordan?"

"They're both good. Which creates a dilemma for the cops. They can't arrest either one if there's an alternate suspect." Zach maneuvered into the left lane so he could pass a bus. "There's something else I've been hesitant to bring up because I know you don't want Jordan to be guilty."

"Go ahead, say it. At this point what I want most is to find out the truth."

"Jordan said he *found* Claudia's body, which doesn't make a hell of a lot of sense. You need to get him to tell you exactly what he did that night."

"I left a message on his voicemail but he hasn't called back."

"When you decide you're going to make somebody talk, you always find a way to do it."

"I'll call him again tonight."

Cassidy sat at her desk and dialed Jordan's number, wondering if he would see her name on his caller I.D. and refuse to answer.

After three rings, the phone was picked up. "I thought you'd get the message when I didn't return that first call," Jordan said, his voice tight with anger.

"I kept my promise. I shredded your records and didn't report your visit."

"You kept your promise," he mimicked nastily. "Then how do you suppose the cops made it to my house by four A.M.? How did they even find out she was dead if you didn't tell them?"

"You think I turned you in?"

"Only four people knew she was dead. The killer, me, you, and your reporter husband—who wrote that story in the *Post*."

Oh shit! Should've realized he'd make the connection.

"How'd you find her body? What reason would you have for being in her house unless you went there to kill her?"

He laughed, not a pleasant sound. "For all you know, she begged me to come back and by the time I got to her place, someone had shot her. If you want the real skinny, get the detectives to tell you.

I explained everything to them and they let me go."
Jordan disconnected.

Cassidy gritted her teeth. *Blaming you after all you went through to protect him.*

She tried to hold on to her indignation but it slipped away. *As much as you want to be pissed, you can't deny it was Zach's call that brought the police down on Jordan. Way sooner than they would have gotten to him otherwise. Giving him less time to pull himself together.*

Cassidy jiggled a pen between her fingers for about three beats, then went into the computer room to see what Zach was up to.

He looked at her as she slid into the chair beside his. "I just came up with an interesting tidbit about Goldstein. Ran him through LexisNexis and discovered he'd been living with his wife in Wilmette until last August, when he moved out of the marital home. Nobody's filed for divorce yet, though."

"This could be totally irrelevant," Cassidy said, not sounding as if she meant it.

"But that's not what you think."

"Well, I can't help but wonder if Paul Goldstein got caught up in the waves of irresistibility Claudia was putting out."

"The same thought crossed my mind. Now all we have to do is get Alyssa Goldstein to tell us why her husband left."

Cassidy swiveled her chair slightly, moving her eyes away from Zach. "I hope we have better luck with her than I did with Jordan."

"You couldn't get him to talk?"

"He thinks I turned him in. And not without reason. Who knows how long it might've been before anyone discovered Claudia was dead if you hadn't made that call."

"Give him a day or so and try again. When it comes to getting what you want, you have a certain irresistibility yourself."

Frowning, she turned to face him. "I wish you'd stop saying things like that.   You set up these expectations, and then if I can't meet them I feel like I've failed."

Zach smiled broadly. "When have you ever *not* met them?   Now don't try to drag me into a discussion of your feelings. It's after seven and we need to drive to Wilmette."

"That's an hour away." Wilmette was a wealthy North Shore suburb with no easy way to get there from Oak Park. "Wouldn't it make more sense to call and set up an interview?"

"I can't think of a single thing I could say on the phone that would get her to give us an interview. But if we're standing on her porch, we may be able to talk our way into her house."

Chapter 33

The wide carved door opened a crack, a chain visible in the gap between the edge of the door and the frame. Zach held his press pass close to the narrow opening. "I'm Zach Moran from the *Post,* and this is my wife, Cassidy. We'd like to talk to you."

"What about?" a woman's voice asked.

"Your husband, Dr. Goldstein."

"Then you should be at his place, not mine."

"I've already spoken with him, but there are a few things I need to find out from you." Zach handed her his press pass.

Alyssa Goldstein opened the door and let them in. "I'm probably going to regret this," she said, her voice surprisingly cheerful. She looked at Cassidy. "You're his wife? Why would a reporter bring his wife?"

"I'm a social worker and I'm doing research for a book on crime victims."

"So that means you're here about Claudia. Of course that was the first thing I thought of." Alyssa was short with a softly curved figure, more maternal than sexual. Her straight chestnut hair hung loosely past her shoulders, and a hint of sadness showed in her light brown eyes, belying the upbeat quality of her voice.

Good at acting like everything's fine when it's not.

Alyssa gave Zach a long look. "I'm sorry, but there's no way I'm going to talk to a reporter about Claudia."

"We can do this off the record," he replied. "That means I couldn't use anything you said."

Alyssa shifted her weight from one foot to the other. She looked down at the tiled floor, then up at the ten-foot ceiling. "I really shouldn't do this," she said, talking more to herself than to them. She turned to Cassidy. "Did you say you were a social worker?"

Cassidy nodded.

"My therapist's a social worker. She's helped me a lot."

Wants to tell her story. Wants me to give her a reason to do it.

"Zach's investigating Claudia's murder.   He needs to learn as much as he can about her.   I think you have a perspective nobody else has."

Alyssa studied Zach's face, as if trying to gauge whether she could trust him. "You guarantee you won't pass on a single thing I tell you?"

"Not one word."

"All right, let's go sit in the living room."

They settled in three of the four easy chairs surrounding a round marble table. The chairs were cushy, with rolled arms and backs and no sharp edges, not unlike the warm, comfortable presence of the woman who owned them. The room was done in shades of honey-beige, the chairs a little darker, the walls a little lighter, the paint giving off a muted glow.

"You want the long version or the short one?" Alyssa asked.

"We've got plenty of time," Zach answered. Leaving his notepad in his pocket, he rested his hands on his thighs.

"It's hard to know where to start."   Alyssa absently picked up an empty mug from the table and turned it around in her hands. "I thought we had a good marriage, better than most. We were still in love after eleven years together. We talked about everything...I thought we were very close. Paul used to tell me about these flings Claudia had. There were times we'd get together socially...I'd have her over for dinner, we'd go to a concert together...." Alyssa stared into the mug. Cassidy could see that she was breathing more rapidly now.

"Then something changed," Cassidy said in the low soothing tone she used with clients.

After several seconds Alyssa picked up her story again. "About a year ago, we started trying to get pregnant. For the first couple of months Paul seemed enthusiastic, then he gradually got more distant and started making excuses not to have sex. I assumed he was having second thoughts. I don't know how many times I tried to talk to him about it but he always brushed me off."

"I hate it when you know something's wrong and you can't get the other person to tell you what it is," Cassidy said, thinking of the times Zach had shut down on her.

Alyssa nodded.

Cassidy waited for her to continue. When she didn't, Cassidy prompted, "So what happened next?"

"He told me...he told me he was in love with Claudia...and wanted a divorce."

"What a shock!"

Alyssa's chin was quivering. She gripped the mug in both hands. "At first I didn't believe it. He knew what she was like. He knew she never stayed with anyone. We used to laugh about her escapades. But then, when he moved out, I knew he really was in love with her."

"You must've felt so betrayed."

"I was livid. I was furious. I wanted to kill both of them. During the first few weeks I couldn't bring myself to tell my friends, but my mother pried it out of me. She just hated him for what he'd done, and the more we talked, the more I hated him too. She kept after me to find a shark of a lawyer and take him for every cent he was worth."

But Alyssa hasn't filed.   "So did you see a lawyer?"

"I had a consultation but I couldn't get myself to take the next step. I felt sort of paralyzed. That's when I started therapy."

"Have you discussed divorce with your husband?" Zach asked.

"After I saw the lawyer, I told Paul I was going to take the house and make him give me maintenance. But I never followed through."

"You're eligible for maintenance?"

"I work for a nonprofit and make next to nothing, so the lawyer said I had a good chance at getting it based on the discrepancy in our incomes."

Zach asked, "What stopped you from going forward with the divorce?"

"Well..." She traced the floral pattern on the mug with one fingernail. "When Paul first moved out, I blamed him. I thought it was his responsibility to stay away from other women. That he should have kept an emotional fence up between him and Claudia like he does with his female patients. And then I started thinking it was her fault—that she had some kind of power over men and she'd just gone after him. That he was this innocent victim. But deep down I knew he wasn't all that innocent. And then I started thinking...." A look of anguish came over Alyssa's face.

"What did you start thinking?" Cassidy asked.

"That for years nothing had happened between them and then it did. That as long as he was happy with me he had no reason to look elsewhere. But then I got so caught up in wanting a baby I must have pressured him too much. Or maybe I wasn't paying attention to him. Or something."

"So you started blaming yourself," Cassidy said.

She wanted to shake Alyssa and scream at her that it wasn't her fault. That wives don't have to be perfect to expect fidelity from their husbands. Forcing herself to speak calmly, she said, "That's why you didn't go ahead with the divorce."

Alyssa swallowed. "I was so confused. One part of me was still furious with Paul and wanted to hurt him financially. Another part thought it was as much my fault as his. And then there was my mother, constantly pushing me to file the papers. I couldn't tell her what I was thinking at all. Thank God I had my therapist to talk to."

"So you've been stuck all this time?"

Chapter 34

Alyssa hunched her shoulders and sighed. "It gets worse. About three months after Paul moved out, he came to me and said it was all over with Claudia and he still loved me and wanted to come home. But I knew Claudia always left first. She just up and left while the men were still crazy about her. So I figured the only reason Paul wanted to come home was that he was sick of living in a crummy apartment and didn't want to lose half his assets in a divorce. I felt insulted. Used. So I was deliberately mean to him."

"But you wanted to believe him."

Alyssa blinked back tears. She pressed her fingers against her eyelids, then lowered her hands into her lap and looked down at them. "I don't see how I could ever trust him again. I'd always feel like I was second best."

Zach shifted in his chair. "Does Paul think you're still planning to go ahead with the divorce?"

"That's what I told him."

"Did he only try that one time?" Cassidy asked. "Did he give up after you were mean to him?"

Alyssa nodded.

God, that must've hurt. What she wanted was for him to prove he loved her by pursuing her even though she was mean. But he failed the test.

"Have the police contacted you?" Zach wanted to know.

"No."

"Do you think your husband could have killed Claudia?"

"If you'd asked me that before he got involved with her, I'd have said it was impossible. I used to think Paul would never hurt anybody. Now I feel like I don't even know him. I have no idea what he might be capable of."

Cassidy said, "You think there's any possibility you might relent and take him back? I've known couples who were able to get past things like this."

Alyssa grinned, her expression becoming jaunty again. "Mom would kill me."

"This isn't her decision."

"You try telling her that."

Although the sky was dark, a hazy mauve glow hung over the city as Zach pulled away from the curb and wheeled south. Cassidy said, "It really got to me, hearing Alyssa tell us about her husband dumping her for another woman after eleven years of being happily married. It's such a reminder that you can never be totally sure of anybody." She twisted her garnet wedding ring.

"Does that mean you think I might get bewitched by another woman and jump ship?"

Your hot button. Before you married Zach, you always thought men were going to leave.

"You know," Zach said, "it could just as easily happen the other way around. You could be the one who gets smitten and runs off with somebody else."

"Not me. I'm loyal to the point of stupidity."

He laughed. "You just said you never can be sure of anybody, and here you are, trying to exempt yourself. But you're absolutely right--there are no guarantees. However, I can't imagine either one of us lusting after someone else." He reached over to squeeze her hand. "So don't lie awake worrying, okay?"

He turned west on Dempster while Cassidy gazed out the side window, going over in her mind what they had learned from Alyssa. The Subaru passed a cyclist who was decked out in dark colors, no reflectors on his bike, no helmet on his head. Cassidy sighed inwardly.

She faced forward.   "I'm amazed Paul would allow himself to get snared by Claudia, considering he knew her track record."

"You fell for me even though you knew I was a jerk when it came to women."

"That's right.   I almost forgot there's a total disconnect between our hormones and our frontal lobes."

Cassidy cranked the heat up a notch.   "So now we have a third guy who might've been pissed off enough to want to kill Claudia."

"She pretty much wrecked his life, so I'd say yeah, Paul had a motive."

"I was surprised the police hadn't gotten to Alyssa before we did."

"The cops already have Jordan and Ray Franklin, two suspects who fell into their laps.   I'd guess they're focusing all their attention on digging up enough evidence to charge one or the other of those two.   They'd have no reason to look at Goldstein."

Zach slowed down.   The car ahead of him, a full-sized sedan with a license plate hanging askew, was driving well under the speed limit, and the small hatchback in the left lane was moving only slightly faster.

"You know," Cassidy said, "I still think there's a strong possibility that Paul committed euthanasia."

"A mercy killing is a whole different animal from murder."

"I suppose, but I can't help thinking that if you've killed once, it'd be easier to kill again."

The next morning Cassidy was sitting up in bed with Starshine on her chest, the cat's eyes slitted, her body vibrating in an exuberant purr. Cassidy scratched the cat's cheek with one fingernail, then picked up her purple mug from the nightstand where Zach had put it and sipped her coffee.

Ever since she'd met Claudia's nephew, she'd been trying not to think about how bad his life was likely to get. But with her mind disengaged, the thoughts she'd tried to avoid were creeping in.

What will David do without money? He can't even get to Hyde Park without bus fare.

He could get a job. But how much can a fifteen-year-old earn? And how much time would he have left for all the things that make his life bearable?

Cassidy considered putting money into an account for him herself. *Not a good idea. He'd feel like a charity case. You'd get overinvolved. Once you took him on, there'd be no way out.*

Still, it couldn't hurt to email him and ask how he's doing.

Zach came into the bedroom. Hopping off Cassidy's chest, Starshine curled up on her desk chair. Zach was already dressed, even though it was only a little after seven. Dressed meant a black tee shirt, black jeans, and black gym shoes.

"Red suspenders—that's what you need."

"I'll leave the color to you. I'm going into work."

"On Saturday?"

"I have to keep up with my other assignments or Libby will yank me off the investigation. I got up early so I could catch Goldstein at home before he left for the clinic. He says they close at one and he'll talk to us after he finishes with his last patient."

"What did it take to get him to agree to see us?"

"I told him I knew he'd left his wife last August and I had a hunch it was because of Claudia. At first he told me to fuck off—my words, not his—but then I said I was going to find out one way or another, so he decided he'd rather tell me himself than have me hear it from somebody else." Zach scooped up his wallet from his desk and stuffed it into his hip pocket. "Why don't I pick you up here around twelve-fifteen?"

"I'm glad we're going back to the clinic. This'll give me a chance to return that photo of Ray Franklin and Claudia to Jill."

Zach left and Cassidy went into the computer room to email David. "How's it going? You must miss hearing from Claudia. Do you have enough money left in your account to maintain your lifestyle? Have you thought about what you'll do when the money runs out?"

She reread the words she'd written. *All wrong. Teenagers hate it when adults feel sorry for them. And when they ask questions.* She stared at the screen for several seconds but couldn't think of anything else to say and so she clicked *send.*

Chapter 35

Cassidy showered, dressed, and went down to the kitchen, Starshine nearly tripping her on the stairs. *Eat yogurt, make sure the client bathroom is clean, go back upstairs and put on lipstick. And you'll have to hurry 'cause Jan shows up early.*

Starshine ran ahead of her into the kitchen and started making strange noises. As Cassidy went through the doorway, she picked up a foul odor. The smell grew stronger as she came around the room divider. The calico, her nose probing the crack beneath the back door, was growling and hissing.

Oh shit! The orange tom's sprayed your door.

Starshine started dancing back and forth as if to say, *Let me at 'im.*

You've gotta scrub the door before Jan gets here. And you've gotta lock Starshine up before you can even open it.

Cassidy grabbed the calico, who fought to get away. *Wants to defend her territory against the outlander who dared to spray her door.* She shut the cat in the basement, took a rag and a bottle of Pinesol, and went out on the stoop. Sitting on her heels, she inspected the bottom of the door. The tom's marking was clearly visible. She applied elbow grease.

A voice came from behind her. "Cassidy?"

She twisted around to see Jan standing at the foot of the steps. A lawyer in her thirties, she was clad in a dark red jacket and skirt with matching three-inch heels. She was the only one of Cassidy's clients who had expressed an aversion to cats.

Cassidy stood, hoping the pine-scented aroma of the cleanser would overpower the stink of the spray.

"A homeless cat marked my door," she explained.

Her client's face registered disgust.

Both sides of the street were lined with cars when Cassidy and Zach arrived at the Edgewater Family Practice.

"There's a lot in back," she said. "That's where I parked when I came to get the picture from Jill." She patted her purse, which held the photo in an envelope.

Zach passed the clinic, turned right at the end of the block, and entered an alley that paralleled the street. He eased the Subaru into a slot next to a black sedan. One other nondescript car was parked in the lot.

Cassidy perused the two cars that were there before them. "That's odd. I wonder if Dr. Goldstein left early to get out of talking to us."

"Huh?"

"He drives a red Porsche. At least I think he does. When I was here before, a Porsche was parked next to these other two cars. I figured the Porsche had to belong to the doctor."

"Let's go check inside." They trekked around to the front and went in through the entrance.

The med tech, in a skin-tight bright orange shirt, smiled at them from behind the counter. "Hey," she said to Zach as they crossed the room, "I remember you. You're the reporter."

Not wanting to be left out, Cassidy jumped in quickly. "We're here to see Dr. Goldstein."

The med tech brushed wisps of reddish burgundy hair out of her eyes. "He should be done in a few minutes."

So where's the Porsche? Maybe it's in the shop and he cabbed it here.

"Is Jill busy?" Cassidy asked. "I'd like to say hello." *And give her the picture.*

"She isn't in today."

Cassidy scrunched her brow. *What? Does that mean the Porsche belongs to Jill? But we talked about it. She said it was dreamy and she didn't say it was hers.*

Before long a patient emerged from the inner office. Paul Goldstein stood in the doorway and beckoned to Cassidy and Zach. They followed the doctor down the corridor and into his office. He sank into the chair behind his desk and Cassidy and Zach sat in front of it. His desktop held only a few file folders and a prescription pad.

The pad jogged Cassidy's memory. *What did he say about prescription pads? Somebody stole one.*

Paul propped his elbows on the desk and buried his face in his hands. "I can't do this."

Zach stood. "Then I'll find somebody else."

He and Cassidy were walking out the door when Paul called after them. "No, wait. I can't let you go asking around about Claudia and me. Yes, we had an affair. And I left my wife because of it. And then we broke up."

Zach turned around. "Sorry. That's not good enough."

Paul looked directly at him for the first time. "What do you want from me?"

They sat down again. "The whole story," Zach said. "Starting with when and how the affair began."

Paul stared into space a moment, then let out a long exhalation of breath. "A year ago. A couple of months after she got rid of that loser who was stalking her. I went into her office one day and was surprised to see her looking upset. It wasn't like her. She had this great optimistic outlook. Whenever I was down, she'd tell me that things usually work out for the best in the long run."

Optimistic? More like Pollyanna-ish.

Cassidy asked, "What about that time when her patient died? Did she take that in stride as well?"

Paul shook his head. "No, of course not. She was very hard on herself for the first few weeks after it happened. But she bounced back faster than I could have. I don't know how many times I heard her say that death is a natural part of life, that everybody has to die sometime, and that the people they leave behind simply have to make the best of it."

"Getting back to how the affair started...," Zach prompted.

Paul rubbed his hand over his bald spot. "When I noticed she was upset, I asked what was wrong. She told me she'd just talked to her nephew and was sure he was holding something back. She worried about him a lot."

"Things usually work out for the best" apparently didn't apply to David.

The doctor added, "So I asked if she'd like to go out after work and talk about it and she said yes."

"Were you hoping more would come of it?" Zach asked.

"Absolutely not. I was in love with my wife. I never imagined I'd get involved with Claudia. I told Alyssa what I was planning to do and she was fine with it."

"So you went out together after work," Cassidy said.

"I remember Claudia mentioning that she could tell Alyssa and I were happy together and that she envied us our marriage. That hit me as ironic because my wife and I were going through a bit of a rough patch at the time."

"What was the problem?" Cassidy asked.

Paul waved dismissively. "Oh, it was nothing. Alyssa was frustrated with me because she wanted us to get pregnant right away and I was hanging back. Anyway, Claudia opened up to me about her intimacy issues and how she didn't see any happy endings in her future. We finished off the first bottle of wine and I ordered a second. The next thing I knew we were both a little tipsy and Claudia was inviting me back to her house."

Cassidy tried to read the expression on Paul's face. She thought it might be shame. "So that was the beginning."

"It was, but I didn't realize it at the time. As soon as the sex was over, I knew I'd made a huge mistake." He picked up the prescription pad and turned it over and over in his slender, long-fingered hands. "I left right away and on the drive home my first impulse was to confess to Alyssa and hope she'd forgive me. But then I convinced myself that the sex was a one-time deal and that I shouldn't inflict pain on Alyssa just to ease my conscience. So I told her the reason I was late was that my pager'd gone off and I had to go into the hospital to see a patient."

Chapter 36

"But obviously it wasn't a one-time deal," Zach said.

"It was like an addiction. I kept telling myself I had to stop but I couldn't. Then, after we'd been sleeping together for a few months, Claudia started saying I was her soulmate. That the reason she hadn't been able to stick with any of the others was that none of them was the one."

"But you were." Zach sat straighter, his body growing slightly more rigid.

Paul nodded.

How gullible can you get? But then, what man could resist being anointed by Claudia as "the one?"

Cassidy cupped her right elbow in her left hand. "How did Claudia feel about the fact that you were married?"

"She didn't say much about it. I got the impression she thought that if she and I belonged together, my marriage to Alyssa had to have been a mistake."

"Did she encourage you to leave your wife?" Zach asked.

Paul sighed. "I suppose you could say that. She talked about us having a future together."

"So why didn't you?" Zach asked. "Have a future with Claudia, I mean."

A tremor passed through the muscles in Paul's cheek. Clearing his throat, he said, "Because I came to my senses and realized I didn't really love her. It was all about the sex. The only person I've ever really loved is Alyssa. So I broke it off with Claudia and went to my wife and tried to get her to take me back. But she wasn't having any of it. So now I guess I'm headed for divorce."

Yeah, right. Out of all the men Claudia's been with, you're the only one who had the sense to leave first.

Cassidy said, "I understand Claudia had a history of suddenly ending relationships. Are you sure she wasn't about to dump you and that's why you broke it off?"

Paul started drumming his fingers on the desk. "Of course I'm sure. Claudia wanted us to be together but I knew it wouldn't work."

Zach said, "Maybe you started thinking about how much you stood to lose in a divorce."

"Look—I told you—I ended my affair because I was still in love with my wife."

Cassidy asked, "How did Claudia take it?"

Paul shrugged. "It was hard on her at first. But like I said, she was quick to bounce back."

"What was it like," Zach asked, "you two working together post breakup?"

"We were friends before the affair and we were able to be friends again afterward."

Cassidy said, "That was very mature of you. But didn't you feel some resentment over Claudia enticing you into an affair that cost you so much?"

He looked at her, and she could see the bitterness in his face even as he shook his head to deny it. "She didn't entice me. We went into it together. And I was the one who cheated, not her. I've got no one to blame but myself."

"Where were you last Tuesday night?" Zach asked.

"Home watching television. While I drank beer and ate take-out from Taco Bell."

Sometimes the things that come around do, in fact, go around.

"So..." Paul took a breath. "Now that I've admitted how badly I screwed up, what are you going to do with the information?"

"If it turns out you had nothing to do with the murder, I'll keep it to myself."

"Claudia and I were on good terms. I had no reason to hurt her."

"Well, then, I guess you have nothing to worry about."

"He was obviously lying," Cassidy said, as Zach backed out of the parking slot.

"You mean the part where he said he dumped Claudia instead of the other way around?"

"She was always the one to break it off."

"You can't possibly know that. And even if she did in every other case, Paul could have been the one exception."

"Oh come on. He left his wife and was willing to give up half his assets to be with Claudia. Is that the kind of guy who'd suddenly decide he wasn't in love with her anymore?"

Braking at a stop sign, Zach turned to study Cassidy's face. "This is about Kevin, isn't it?"

A horn blared behind him and he started moving again.

"What are you saying?"

"You know exactly what I'm saying. Kevin cheated on you, so naturally you identify with Alyssa and see Paul as a lying piece of shit."

Cassidy refused to look at her husband. "I *know* he was lying when he said he didn't feel resentful. It was written all over his face."

Zach didn't say anything.

"What? You think he was telling the truth?"

"No, I think you're probably right. The odds are he is lying, but we can't know for sure. The other thing is, I don't consider his lying to be particularly significant. Why would you expect him to admit that Claudia led him on, ruined his marriage, then dumped him. That would make him both a chump and an instant suspect. If I were in his place, I'd lie too."

"He has just as strong a motive as Jordan or Franklin."

"So why now?" Zach asked. "If Claudia dumped him several months ago, why wait this long to get revenge?"

"There could be all kinds of reasons we wouldn't know about. And I'm not against him just because of Kevin. I thought he was guilty of euthanasia after we talked to him that first time."

"So now we have three viable suspects. Two more than we need."

As the Subaru rolled along the north side of their house, Cassidy noticed a yellowed sheet of newspaper that had blown up against their chain link fence. Zach parked near the gate and they both got out. She paused on the sidewalk, her gaze bouncing from the red McDonald's French fry carton on the parkway grass to the dirty gym shoe nestled in the weeds that grew up around the bottom of the fence.

Litter accumulates in your yard even faster than you can empty bags of peanut butter cups.

Cleaning up usually falls on Zach's shoulders. But since you claim to be a feminist, you really ought to take your turn.

She decided to attend to the litter problem after she checked to see if David had replied to her email. She signed on and scanned her new messages. One of them was from madscntst. "U don't need 2 worry about me. I'll b ok. There r plenty of job opportunities in Stone Park.   I can apprentice with the Latin Kings and learn the car jacking biz."

Well, what did you expect?   That exchanging emails would somehow make things better?

Or maybe you were hoping he wouldn't answer and that would let you off the hook.

She didn't want to talk to Zach about it because he would tell her it wasn't her problem.   But he would be wrong.   She was the only responsible adult who knew how grim David's situation was and that meant she had to do something about it.

Zach walked up behind her.   "We're going to have to become a two-computer household so neither of us has to wait in line."

She logged off and turned the chair over to him. "You're just looking for an excuse to buy another computer."

"I don't need an excuse."

Chapter 37

She went down to the kitchen, got out a garbage bag, and put on latex gloves. Outside, the sun beat down at an angle and the shadows had started to lengthen. She was bending over to pick up a smashed soda can when an idea came to her. *David has a grandmother. A grandmother who may already feel some guilt over her refusal to take him when he was a baby. Maybe you can crank it up enough to get her to put money in his account.*

Cassidy spotted several small items in the weeds between the hydrangea bushes that grew along the north side of the house. She squatted and reached for one, then realized it was a used condom. Her hand stopped in midair. *For God's sakes, you've got gloves on.* She deposited the condom in her bag, stood up, and gazed at the vehicles lining the curb. *Do couples actually do it right here in their cars? Where pedestrians can see them? When you were messing around in backseats, you'd never have had the nerve to copulate in such a public place.*

She got down on one knee and continued pulling litter out of the weeds. A small white dog, floppy ears, curly tail, trotted up and probed her hand with its nose.

"This isn't anything you want to eat."

"Hello there," came a deep voice from behind her.

Standing, she peeled off one of her gloves and brushed her cinnamon hair back from her face. "How you doing?" she said to her neighbor, a portly man with dark brown skin and grizzled white hair.

"I'm good, I'm good." His voice was so resonant, his creased slacks and polished shoes so proper, she always imagined him to be a retired minister or judge.

"This is the first time I've seen you this spring," he added.

Cassidy grimaced. "I need a dog. It would get me out more. It would also force me to get some exercise."

"I'm sure you know how important it is to stay fit. I've got a rowing machine and I use it everyday."

Edward Fremont was the chatty type. He would keep talking until she excused herself and went inside. She had a limited tolerance for idle conversation, but whenever she ran into him she gave him a few minutes of her time because he seemed lonely.

"I'm glad I caught you." He picked up the fluffy white dog and cradled it in his arms. "I've seen this man sitting in a banged-up old car a couple of times. Once I went all the way around the block and he was still there. Seems to me anybody who's just sitting in his car is up to no good. Probably something to do with drugs."

"You didn't call the police?"

"I don't have a cell phone. And he wasn't breaking any laws." The dog reached up to lick Fremont's chin.

"Doesn't matter. The cops want citizens to report any suspicious activity. If you run across this guy again, you should go straight home and call the police. Whatever he's up to, they'll discourage him from doing it in Oak Park."

Fremont shook his head. "I've been in my apartment for three years now and I still don't have the hang of how things work here. When I lived in the city, most folks wouldn't think of calling the police."

"It's different here." Cassidy shifted her weight. "Thanks for telling me about the guy in the car. I'll keep my eyes out for him." She looked at her watch. "Ooops, it's getting late. Time I went inside and started dinner."

Cassidy sailed through the kitchen and went upstairs. Cooking was the last thing on her mind. *No way you can even think about planning a meal when there are so many more interesting things to do.*

She sat at her desk and looked up Ellen's number in her notepad. She pictured the businesswoman in her navy pantsuit and freshly applied makeup. *Wouldn't talk about Hailey, practically pushed us out the door.* Cassidy realized that getting Ellen to finance her grandson's lifestyle might be a tough sell. *Four o'clock Saturday afternoon. She's probably running errands. Or getting ready to meet someone for dinner. Better to call first thing tomorrow morning.*

Cassidy was attempting to bring some order to her desk when Zach came into the room. "Someone named Gwen Dickert called while you were out." He stuck a post-it with a number on it on her desk.

"Gwen Dickert." Cassidy tilted her head, trying to remember who she was. "The woman whose mother was euthanized by Paul Goldstein."

"The nutcase who claims her mother was euthanized."

Cassidy scowled at her husband. "Go away. I don't want you laughing at me while I'm on the phone."

"How 'bout if I only smirk?"

"Get out of here."

Zach left and Cassidy dialed the number.

"I was thinking today about all that time you spent with me after I got so upset at Dr. G's office, and I wanted you to know that talking to you helped settle me down. So I called to tell you that, and then there's this other thing I thought you might be interested in."

"I'm glad I was able to help." *Here she thinks you were being nice and your real agenda was to pump her for information.*

"You gave me time to tell the whole story. Nobody else ever does that. My husband never listens and my friend always tells me what to do. You were a complete stranger but I felt like you cared."

So what's the real reason she called? Seems like she's asking for another small dose of therapy.

"How's it going, dealing with your mother's death?"

"Just terrible. I can't seem to stop crying. My husband hates it when I break down in front of him. And my friend keeps telling me I should put it behind me. She looked up some stuff on the Internet and told me I should go to a grief group. Said it'd help me move on. So I went to two different groups last week but I still keep falling apart."

"Your mother must've been very important to you."

"Ever since her accident I've been taking care of her. It was the first time in my life I felt like I was doing something useful."

"So you lost your mother, her companionship, and your sense of purpose. That's a lot of losses. It takes most people a long time to recover from something as devastating as that. And crying is one of the best ways to do it. God gave us tears so we could let our feelings out."

"You don't think it's so bad that I keep crying all the time?"

"I think it's really healthy. But a lot of men don't understand that we need time to grieve.

"Well, I'm going to tell my husband you said that."

And then he'll make some crack about how wacky therapists are.

"Oh," Gwen said, "there's one other thing. I was at a grief group and an older woman talked about her brother. Said she was sure someone helped him die. After the group was over, I told her I'd been through the same thing. But then she said something that really put me off. Said he wanted to die and she didn't have the courage to help him but she was glad someone else did. She obviously wasn't a Christian and I didn't want to talk to her after that. But I did ask who her brother's doctor was because I thought maybe Dr. G killed two people. Turns out it was a different doctor, though."

"That's very interesting," Cassidy remarked, not knowing what else to say.

"You wanted to hear all about Dr. G killing my mother so I thought you might want to talk to this other woman too."

"Thanks for thinking of me."

"I took her name and number in case you want to get in touch with her."

"Uh...sure. Go ahead and give it to me."

Cassidy jotted the information down, then brought the conversation to a close. *How strange. Is there an epidemic of euthanasia going around? Or is this just a coincidence?* Zach said he didn't believe in coincidences but Cassidy knew they did in fact occur.

She gazed at the name she'd written in her notepad and wondered if there was any reason to follow up. *This woman has no apparent connection* to Claudia or Paul Goldstein.   I can't see how it would do any good to call her.

Chapter 38

Cassidy took the chair next to Zach's at the computer table. "Let's go to Cucina's." Cucina Paradiso was an Italian restaurant located on the fringes of Oak Park's restaurant row.

"Okay," Zach said, his eyes never leaving the screen.

"We have to hurry. It'll be packed by seven."

When they arrived, a few tables were still empty, including the one near the wall on the left, which they usually grabbed. As they sat down, Cassidy's eyes were drawn to a glowing orange panel on the opposite side of the room, part of the striking new décor that had graced the interior when the restaurant reopened after a fire. A tall attractive waitress came over right away.

"So, what are you two up to?" she asked, looking at Zach.

"Just the usual," Zach said.

"Another investigation? A murder? I wish I could pry some of the details out of you."

"Most of what I do is pretty routine. If this case I'm working on ever breaks, you can read about it in the *Post*."

Cassidy doubted that the young woman, who'd told them about her two preschoolers, spent much time reading the paper. *So many people who don't read papers. So many papers going under.* She pushed away the thought, which, if she dwelt on it, would trigger twitches of anxiety in her stomach.

Zach ordered a bottle of Pinot Noir and the waitress went to fetch it.

"I'm going to try to guilt Claudia's mother into depositing money into David's account," Cassidy said.

"She ought to be willing to do at least that much."

"I'm not so sure. Remember how she refused to talk about Hailey and David?"

Zach broke off a slice of Italian bread and dunked it into olive oil and parmesan cheese. "I guess mothers usually try to keep it a secret when their kids screw up. They probably expect everyone to blame them for their kid's bad behavior."

"Actually, they tend to blame themselves. That's the real reason they don't want anyone to know."

"But they're perfectly happy to claim bragging rights when their kids succeed. Take your mother, for instance. I bet she's really proud of you."

Cassidy wrinkled her nose. "If she is, she never tells me."

"She doesn't want it to go to your head."

Cassidy examined Zach's face. He appeared not to have any feelings on the topic of mothers. It was amazing to her that he had emerged as a reasonably healthy person after being raised by a mother who never wanted anything to do with him. *And without a single therapy session. If everyone were as resilient as Zach, you'd be out of business.*

The waitress returned and poured their wine, then took their orders.

"It's a shame Mildred never allowed herself to take pride in your success," Cassidy said.

"She needs to think of me as a fuck-up so she can justify her dislike of me."

"But wouldn't it be nice if she could recognize your achievements?"

He shook his head. "If she did, you'd probably pressure me to have some sort of relationship with her. I'm fine with things the way they are." He grinned. "And so are you, because you don't like her any better than I do."

On Sunday morning Cassidy finished the coffee Zach had put on her nightstand, then picked up her desk phone.

"This is Cass McCabe," she said after Ellen answered. "I'd like to talk to you about your grandson."

"Cass McCabe?" She sounded vague, as if she didn't remember.

Pretending she doesn't know who you are.

"I was with my husband, Zach Moran, when he interviewed you."

"Oh...yes."

"I felt that somebody needed to tell your grandson, David, about Claudia's death, so I hunted him down and gave him the news. We did quite a bit of talking and there are some things I thought you'd want to know about him." *Even if she doesn't, she's not likely to say so.*

"Well, I have to leave soon...but go ahead and tell me."

"I don't mean now. I want to set up a time when we can sit down and talk in person."

"Whatever you have to say, you can tell me on the phone." Her tone went from vague to irritated.

"I really don't want to do this over the phone. Just tell me what would be a good time and I'll come to your condo."

"I'm very busy."

"I can be in and out in less than half an hour."

Ellen gave an exasperated huff. "If you insist. I'll be home by nine tonight. You can come then."

The front doorbell rang. Cassidy was wiping up crumbs from her lunch and Zach was off shopping for a new techy gadget. As she passed through the living room, she looked out her picture window and saw two men in suits standing in front of the screen door that opened onto her enclosed porch. Her stomach sank. *Cops.*

She crossed the porch and opened the screen door. One man had light brown skin and was in his thirties. The other was white and looked as if he was counting down the months to his retirement.

The older man spoke. "I'm Detective Hobart and this"—he jerked his head toward his partner—"is Detective Crupek. Are you Cassidy McCabe?"

She nodded.

"We'd like to talk to you."

She knew that legally she could refuse to speak to them but that doing so would only make them come after her harder.

"All right."

She let them in, noting the macho swing of Crupek's shoulders. He wore a gold stud in one ear, had a small goatee, and was clad in an expensive, hip-looking suit. Hobart, lumbering behind him, had a fleshy face and a paunch that hung over his belt.

They seated themselves in the living room. The older cop said, "We understand you and your husband have been talking to people who knew Dr. Leavitt."

"Zach's a crime reporter. He's investigating a murder."

Hobart held a stained handkerchief to his mouth and let out a long hacking cough. Annoyance flickered across his partner's face.

"That doesn't explain why you've been going with him on his interviews," Crupek said.

"I'm working on a book."

"Oh really?"   The younger cop raised an eyebrow. "What's it about?"

"Crime victims."

"And what was your excuse the last time you and your husband interfered with a police investigation? And the time before that?"

Seems like every cop in the CPD has heard about your notorious past.

She drew herself up. "I don't believe I want to continue this conversation."

Hobart's tired brown eyes met hers.   "Police never like it when civilians get in their business, but if Moran wants to take you with him, there's nothing we can do about it."

What?   Cops usually yell at you and threaten you with obstruction.

"We also understand that Jordan Wenzlaff was a client of yours," Crupek said. "And that he was seeing you when Dr. Leavitt took out her order of protection."

From Crupek's expression, Cassidy could tell he didn't like her. *Maybe thinks you should've been able to stop Jordan from harassing her.   Or maybe just doesn't like shrinks.*

She said, "I can't discuss him with you."

Hobart let out another death-rattle cough. "A young woman was brutally killed. The fact that you've been talking to suspects indicates that you'd like to find out who murdered her. We're all rowing in the same direction here. Naturally you want to protect your former client, but if you could let us know something about his state of mind when he got slapped with the order, it could help us get closer to an arrest."

"I expect you know almost as much about the rules of confidentiality as I do."

"We're not asking for your records or anything," Hobart said. "We'd just like to get your opinion on whether Wenzlaff is the kind of guy to go from stalking to murder."

"I don't think you heard me."

"Oh, we heard you all right," Crupek said. "We also know actions speak louder than words. And what your actions are telling us is, you think Wenzlaff killed her. The only reason for you to be so involved in this investigation is to try to find out for sure."

"You couldn't be more wrong." She stood. "I'd like you to leave now."

Chapter 39

"I kept expecting them to threaten me with a subpoena," Cassidy said to her husband. They were sitting in their side-by-side leather chairs in the den upstairs. Cassidy had just finished telling Zach about her encounter with the police.

"Sounds like you're off the hook." Zach rested his feet on the footstool.

"But why didn't they threaten to subpoena my records or my testimony?"

"They were on a fishing expedition, probably hoping you'd feel some sense of obligation to get your homicidal ex-client off the street. They couldn't get a subpoena because they didn't have anything to take to a judge. Or maybe therapist-client privilege is so sacred cops don't even try to break it."

"If that's the case, why didn't you tell me at the beginning when I was so worried about getting subpoenaed?" She twisted the footstool around so she could reach it too.

"I said maybe. I haven't run into anything like this before. I don't know what kind of legal protections there are for therapists. When it comes to journos, the situation isn't clearcut. It's rare for courts to subpoena reporters to reveal their sources, but a few have landed in jail for refusing to do it."

"Well...." Cassidy sighed. "Seems like most of the things I worry about never happen."

"Can I get you a glass of wine?" Ellen inquired.

Cassidy, seated in a green wingback chair in front of a wooden coffee table, accepted the older woman's offer.

Without asking whether Cassidy would prefer red or white, Ellen breezed into the kitchen. She returned and handed Cassidy a glass of red, then sat across from her, her own wineglass already on the table. When Cassidy had seen Ellen before, there were signs of grief on the woman's face. Today, Cassidy detected a certain brittleness beneath the well-applied makeup.

"So tell me, why was it so important to pressure me into meeting you in person rather than simply saying what you have to say over the phone?"

Cassidy rubbed her thumb against the smooth fabric of the chair's armrest. "Because despite the fact that David's life has been a complete train wreck, he's a good responsible kid and he needs your help. And I didn't think I could convince you to give it to him over the phone."

"No, I'm sure you couldn't. And I doubt you'll be able to do it in person, either."

Cassidy softened her voice. "But you do want to hear about him, don't you? About the clever ways he's managed to survive, even though his mother is a junkie and she's living with a really mean drug-dealer boyfriend?"

Ellen took a large swallow of wine. "Now that you've pushed your way in here, I suppose I might as well let you have your say."

Cassidy told David's grandmother about his weight lifting, his martial arts, and his aspirations to become a scientist. She also described how he'd had to protect himself from the boyfriend and the means he'd devised to spend most of his time in Hyde Park.

"But he won't be able to do any of those things without money. And that's what I'm here to ask you for. You wouldn't need to have any personal contact.　Just deposit a check in his bank account every month the way Claudia did."

Ellen gave a cynical laugh.　"You make it sound so simple.　But things never are.　And you should be smart enough to know that."

"Why wouldn't it be?"

"Because first I'd start putting money in his account.　Then he'd turn sixteen and tell me he had to have a car to get back and forth between Stone Park and Hyde Park.　And then there'd be insurance and gas money.　And at some point he'd probably get arrested and want me to put up bail and hire an attorney.　Or he'd get addicted or join a gang and everybody would expect me to somehow come to the rescue."

She's reading your mind.　Those are the same fears you have for him.　And some of the reasons you don't want to take responsibility.

Cassidy said, "All you have to do is make it clear he won't receive another cent if he tries to take advantage.　As long as you set clear boundaries, he won't be able to suck you in."

"You don't have children, do you?"

"I have a stepson."

"It's not the same."　Ellen rotated her wineglass in a slow circle.　"I'm sorry, but I'm not willing to do what you want."

What's the matter with her?　Doesn't she have one iota of feeling for her own flesh and blood?

Ellen met Cassidy's eyes.　"Oh, I know what you're thinking.　You think I'm cold and heartless. You're judging me just like Claudia did.　She didn't even try to understand."

"Understand what?"

"Is this your attempt to do therapy on me?"

"No, I'd genuinely like to understand what went wrong between you and Claudia."

Chapter 40

Ellen turned her head away and stared out the wide arched window overlooking the lake. Following her gaze, Cassidy could see sparkling little boat lights in the distance.

After several seconds, Ellen looked at Cassidy again, a glimmer of moisture in her eyes. "My husband never got around to buying life insurance, so when he died I was left with nothing but a stack of medical bills and I hadn't worked outside the home since Claudia was born. I was lucky to get an entry- level job that paid enough to keep us in our house and put food on the table. Claudia was a strong independent kid and she accepted that I couldn't stay home any more, but Hailey was younger and needier. She was so angry she'd barely speak to me."

"God, that must've been awful."

"I was exhausted, overwhelmed. I didn't have anything to give anybody. So you can imagine how thankful I was when Claudia stepped up and started taking care of Hailey. Not only that, but she really seemed to enjoy the role of second mother. And before long Hailey started going to her instead of me. The first few years everything seemed to be fine."

"Then what happened?" *As if you didn't know.*

"Hailey got completely out of control and Claudia told me I had to reign her in. I tried. I sent her to counseling. I took away all her privileges. But the more I tried to restrict her, the wilder she got. Then she turned up pregnant and moved in with her boyfriend. Claudia never said it was my fault, but I could see in her face that she blamed me. We'd always been extremely close and then she turned against me. She just went her own way and acted as if I wasn't even there. I made every attempt I could to win her back but I never did. I lost both my daughters, and I'm not going to start caring about my grandson and then lose him too. And if I send a monthly check, sooner or later I'll want to see him and then.... I'm not going to risk it."

"So you're saying you have to protect yourself. That you can't let yourself have feelings for anybody because they might leave you, the way your husband and daughters did."

"I expect David already heard from Claudia what a terrible person I am."

"That's possible. It's also possible he might break your heart by turning self-destructive like Hailey did."

Cassidy saw the rigidity in Ellen's body ease a little. *You agreed with her so now she doesn't have to be so defensive.*

"The problem is," Cassidy went on, "if you don't give him the money and his life falls apart, you'll never know whether that monthly check might've made the difference. If you do give him the money and he screws up, you'll know the fault was his, not yours."

Cassidy picked up her glass, took a sip of wine, allowed her eyes to roam around the perfectly appointed room, then looked at Ellen again. "I think you've been through a great deal of pain and you've done the best you could to move past it. I also think that if you throw a lifeline to David, a small possibility exists of having a second chance at family. But it must feel very risky to get your hopes up."

Ellen leaned back and briefly closed her eyes. Then she opened them and stood up. Cassidy got to her feet also.

"I'm extremely tired," Ellen said. "I can't think about this any more tonight. I'll call and let you know what I decide."

Cassidy cruised along Briar toward her house, located on the southeast corner of Hazel and Briar. Two lanky teenagers of indeterminate gender crossed Hazel, walking toward her. Briar was illuminated by a streetlamp on the corner and a second streetlamp across from her garage, which stood next to the alley. She drove through the intersection and passed a minivan parked on her side of the street. The only other vehicle on her side was a dark sedan parked almost half a block away from the intersection, its nose snugged up against her driveway.

It was ten-thirty. Her second floor windows were all alight, a testimony to her inability to teach Zach to turn off switches behind him. Cassidy doubted that she was as fatigued as Ellen, but she felt drained from her efforts to change the other woman's mind.

I'll get Zach to sit in bed with me and rub my neck. Maybe even indulge in another glass of wine.

Punching the garage door opener, she glanced at the rear-end of the sedan. She noticed a broken taillight, then skimmed the bumper sticker: *Fuck the pigs.*

Chapter 41

She pulled into her driveway, stopped her car, and suddenly felt a flash of alarm. She jammed her Toyota into reverse, hit the accelerator, and jerked her car back out onto the street. She heard a thunk, like a hammer pounding metal, from somewhere on the passenger side.

Throwing her car into drive, she hurtled toward the alley. The Toyota was headed straight toward a parked crossover on her left, so she yanked hard on the steering wheel to turn the Toyota to the right. The screech of breaking glass sounded from the rear of her car. She twisted around and saw that her back window was shattered.

The Toyota smashed into something, then came to a shuddering halt. Sucking in air, she stared at her crumpled hood. Her car had plowed into the side of her neighbors' garage. *Oh God, he's got you cornered.*

She fumbled with her seatbelt buckle, opened the door, and tumbled out. She took a quick look over her shoulder, expecting the shooter to be standing right behind her, but no one was there.

Her first impulse was to run down the alley, but it was as well lit as the street, so she plunged around to the other side of her neighbors' garage, where she could take cover in the shadows. In front of her stood a six-foot wooden fence with a gate that led into her neighbors' yard. If the gate was latched, she'd have nowhere to go.

Maybe he's gone. Maybe the crash scared him off.

And maybe he's coming after you.

Breathing in short gasps, barely able to think, she pushed the gate to her neighbors' property and it swung inward. She bolted toward their back door, then realized she should have latched the gate behind her. As she started to dash back, a dark figure stepped into the yard. She raced toward the southeast corner of the lot, where two trees cast a dense shadow. She heard a sharp snap, which she instinctively knew was a bullet flying past her. She burrowed in behind a large clump of bushes, the branches digging into her skin. She sat on the spiky ground and willed herself to remain absolutely still. Clamping a hand over her mouth, she forced herself to take deep silent breaths, but there was nothing she could do to quiet the thudding of her heart.

She saw a flash of light and heard the whap of a bullet hitting the fence next to her shoulder. The figure, broad shouldered, medium height, wearing a ski mask, moved into the shadow of the trees and took another shot.

"Cass, hey Cass, where are you?" Zach, a note of panic in his voice, calling from the other side of their neighbor's garage.

The gunman ran out of the yard.

"Hey, you! Stop!" Zach's voice again.

Cassidy started to shake all over. She grabbed a branch and tried to pull herself to her feet but her knees gave way. She was panting so hard she couldn't even speak.

Sirens wailed in the distance.

Zach came through the gate, another man behind him, and looked around.

She choked out a couple of words. "Over here." She tried to stand up again and this time succeeded.

Zach was instantly beside her, his arms gathering her in. "That fucking asshole!"

"Is she all right?" A familiar voice from behind Zach's shoulder.

Two adults and a gang of teenagers poured out of their neighbors' house and crowded around them, all shouting questions at once.

Cassidy heard tires screeching, doors slamming, a garbled mix of voices and the staticky sound of police radios. Two uniformed cops escorted Cassidy, Zach, and the other person, a man who lived across the alley from them, out of the yard. They stopped near Cassidy's wrecked Toyota and one of the cops asked what happened.

The man from across the alley responded first. "I was taking out the garbage when I saw that a car had crashed into the Stein's garage so I rang Zach's bell and asked if it was one of theirs."

Zach, still holding a shaking Cassidy, said, "When he told me it was a Toyota, I knew it had to be Cass's and since she hadn't come inside, I assumed she was still in it. So I called nine-one-one, then came out here and saw that the car was empty. I started yelling for her and this guy dressed all in black came running out of our neighbors' yard."

The second cop looked at Cassidy. "Are you injured? Should I get the paramedics over here?"

"No, he missed." She tried to explain but her story came out all jumbled.

The second cop interrupted her. "I'm going to take you over to one of the squads and give you some time to calm down."

Means I have to sit there till they drive me to the station and take my statement.

The other cop said to Zach, "Might be a good idea for you to wait in a squad car too."

"When I read that bumper sticker," Cassidy said, "it didn't consciously register. I just panicked and tried to get away."

They were sitting in the waterbed, Cassidy leaning her back against Zach's bent knees, his hand slowly massaging her neck. Two glasses of wine sat atop the bookcase headboard. Celine Dion's voice was issuing from the DVD player, Cassidy's choice of music, not Zach's.

"Thank God you did," he said. "If you'd put the car in the garage, there would've been a nine millimeter pointed at your chest when you came out."

"It wasn't until I was giving my statement that I remembered why the bumper sticker scared me."

Zach said, "That old lady with the dog who lived down the street from Claudia. When she told us about a man sitting in a car with that bumper sticker on it, I thought it was her dementia talking."

"So this same guy must've killed Claudia, then tried to kill me." Cassidy turned it over in her mind. "Or maybe not. Claudia's murder was obviously personal and I can't see her getting involved with a guy who has a 'Fuck the Pigs' bumper sticker."

"Me either." Zach removed his hand from Cassidy's neck and twisted around to reach for his wineglass. "I think this guy was a hired gun and a pretty boneheaded one at that. A good hit man never drives his own car, and he certainly doesn't go tooling around with an identifiable bumper sticker."

"Seems to me he was taking a big risk following me after I crashed. Anybody could have heard it and called the cops. In fact, I'm surprised you didn't."

"I did hear something but I thought it was the TV. By all odds, he should've been caught. He left his car facing a cul-de-sac, went into a back yard where he could've been seen from the house, and got away only seconds before the cops arrived. The only smart thing he did was use a silencer. This is the first one I've run into. I thought they only existed in the movies."

Air from the open windows had a chill to it. Cassidy, wearing only a short nightshirt, pulled a purple lap rug over her shoulders and arms. "If he hadn't used a silencer, half the people on the block would've heard the shots and called it in. Even my chatty friend Edward Fremont might've been willing to call the police."

"Claudia told everybody she was going on vacation, so I think the killer hired this mope to keep track of her whereabouts, then hired him again to murder you."

"Claudia didn't tell everybody. She certainly wouldn't have told Jordan."

"Who knows? Maybe Jordan stayed on his good behavior long enough for Claudia to decide they could be friends. A lot of women have this moronic fantasy that they can dump a guy and keep the friendship. That might explain his presence in her house."

"No it doesn't. The killer broke in, remember? Besides, if the killer hired someone to follow Claudia, that means the murder was premeditated and that wasn't Jordan's style. His MO was to act out impulsively." *Except for his urge to shoot her. That was an image he brooded over for a while.*

A resonant baritone voice singing a bluesy riff drifted up from the street. The sound was so compelling they stopped talking and listened until it disappeared in the distance.

"Okay," Zach said, "let's come at this from the other end. There'd be no reason for anybody to kill either one of us unless we know something the cops don't. That wouldn't be true of Franklin. I expect the police have extracted lots more information from him than we have. It would be true of Paul Goldstein. As far as we know, the cops haven't tumbled to his affair with Claudia yet. And then there's Jordan."

Cassidy clenched her back teeth. "Go ahead—say it."

"You know what I'm thinking."

She drew in a breath. "I'm the one who listened to Jordan describe his fantasy of shooting Claudia. I'm the one he's pissed at because he thinks we turned him in." She paused. "And Jordan is the only one who'd be likely to go after me instead of you."

"But at the same time, Jordan probably didn't know about Claudia's vacation and he isn't the premeditation type." Zach finished his wine. "We're going in circles. It's time to give it up and go to sleep."

Chapter 42

Cassidy, behind the wheel of her Toyota, careened through Oak Park, the village so dark it looked as if a blackout had occurred. Zigzagging from one block to another, she turned into a dead end street. As she approached the cul-de-sac, a figure appeared holding a gun out in front of him.

Her eyes flew open. Her body ached, her forehead was covered in sweat.

A short time later she was sitting up in bed, Starshine bundled on her lap, drinking coffee. Her chest was tight and she was gulping in short rapid breaths. She didn't see the room around her. She saw the man coming through her neighbors' gate.

Zach's footsteps jolted her back to reality. He sat down at his desk and swiveled to face her. "How you doing?"

"Not so good." Starshine said *mwat,* coaxing Cassidy to scratch beneath her chin.

"What's wrong?"

Her mind was swirling. She made an effort to focus, then said, "I'm having a reaction to being shot at. A little PTSD." Cassidy's fingers rubbed the calico in exactly the right spot, producing a resounding purr. "If I process it right away, I should recover quickly."

"What do you need to do?"

"I think I'll set up an appointment with Maggie." Maggie was a close friend and fellow therapist.

Therapists aren't supposed to treat people they know.

But Maggie will get you in today, and as long as it's a one-shot deal, she won't have a problem with it.

"I can drive you there," Zach said. "I'm going to stay home and take care of the insurance and get the Toyota towed. After your session we can rent you a car."

Maggie opened the door to her office. "Oh, what an awful experience!" She had heard a condensed version of Cassidy's story over the phone. Throwing her arms around her friend, Maggie said, "Thank goodness you weren't hurt!"

"I was lucky. No damage on the outside. If there's anything I hate, it's emergency rooms."

Three of the office walls were peach, the fourth a floor-to-ceiling bookcase. A desk in one corner. A tan sofa and four chairs, peach and tan stripes, arranged in a circle. Cassidy took the sofa and Maggie sat across from her.

"So what kind of symptoms are you having?" Maggie, a slender woman with a pretty face devoid of makeup, wore a beige shirt and pants. Everything about her was plain except her long silver earrings, which made soft tinkling noises whenever she moved her head.

"A nightmare last night. Heavy duty anxiety. Every now and then I get these flashes of a man shooting at me."

"Pretty much what you'd expect after the ordeal you went through last night."

"You're normalizing."

Maggie smiled. "Why don't you pretend you're a client instead of a therapist."

"I'll try."

"We can't deal with all the aspects of your PTSD in one session."

"Well, but I think my case is fairly minor. One session might be enough."

"That would be nice."   Maggie tilted her head, causing her earrings to make slight chimey sounds. "First I'd like you to tell me everything that happened last night. In detail. If you start to get scared, we'll take a break for a while and come back to it."

Cassidy made it through her entire story with two brief pauses.

Maggie said, "That was good. You seem calmer now than when you talked to me on the phone."

"I feel better just being here."

"Now I'd like you to concentrate on the fears underlying the anxiety."

Cassidy nodded.

Doing this exactly right.   It's the anxiety that causes a lot of the other symptoms.

Stop that! You're supposed to be a client.

Maggie said, "Tell me all the things you're afraid of."

"That the guy who tried to kill me will try again. And that next time he'll succeed. Or kill Zach." Her mouth went dry. "That he'll sit in his car and watch our house. Follow me around." Her voice was shaking.

"Take some deep breaths. Don't say anything more until you feel calmer."

Cassidy did as she was told. When she spoke again, her voice was steady.   "I'm afraid this humungous orange cat will hurt Starshine. And that my client killed his ex." A pause. "And that I'll screw up Zach's investigation...I can't think of anything else."

"You've faced some scary situations before. There've been other times when your life was at risk. How did you manage those previous fears?"

"I...uh...I talked about them with Zach. And I didn't let myself dwell on them. I focused on something else—usually on solving the problem."

"What's different now?"

Cassidy's voice rose a notch. "I almost got killed!"

"But this isn't the first time."

Narrowing her eyes, Cassidy gazed into space. *This really isn't different. So why aren't you using your coping skills?* Something clicked into place in her mind.

"It was the nightmare, the flashback and the anxiety coming on top of each other before I was completely awake. It was just too much at once and I forgot that I know how to handle things like this. But now I remember what I need to do."

"These are PTSD symptoms you're talking about."

"Yes, I know. But I caught it right away and I feel so much more grounded now that I've told my story and separated out the different fears. I really think I'll be okay."

"So you're not going to take my advice and work with a different therapist for a while?"

"You didn't seriously think I would, did you?"

They argued for a few minutes over whether Maggie would allow Cassidy to pay, which she didn't. Then they hugged again and Cassidy left.

Cassidy waited on the corner of Lake and Marian Street for Zach to pick her up. Behind her stood the Cozi Corner Coffee Shop, and three floors above the coffee shop was Maggie's office.

The Subaru pulled up and Cassidy got in. "I want to rent a red Prius."

"Red? This is just a rental. What difference does the color make?"

You really want to be so difficult? Yes, I do. I may not be zingy enough for a Porsche, but I can definitely see myself in a sweet red Prius.

She said, "It may take a while before we can find a red Prius to buy and I don't want to wait. I've been driving a beige car for twelve years and I hate beige. The only reason I bought that car was it was so cheap."

"Then why the hell have you been fighting me all this time about buying a new one?"

"I didn't have a good excuse to get rid of it. It never gave me any trouble and I couldn't justify spending all that money."

"I don't get why it's so hard for you to buy things just because you want them."

"There's nothing wrong with being thrifty."

They went home and Cassidy called around until she found a rental agency that had a red Prius on its lot.

Tuesday afternoon, two weeks since Claudia's murder, the red Prius sat in the garage, Zach was at work, and Cassidy had just finished lunch.

So where do we go from here? She sat in her leather chair in the den, her elbow on the armrest, the side of her face resting against her hand. *We've got three good suspects and no way to narrow them down. And somebody tried to kill me and we don't know why.*

She picked up a legal pad from the side table and wrote "Unfinished Business" at the top. The first item she put on the list was "Get Jordan to tell you how he found Claudia's body." The second was "Get Ray Franklin to tell you about his relationship with Claudia." Remembering that she still had the picture of Franklin and Claudia, she added, "Return photo to Jill."

Then she combed through her notepad looking for anything that might be considered a loose end. She included two more items at the bottom of her list: "Find out about stolen prescription pad" and "Talk to woman Gwen Dickert met at grief group."

Inducing Jordan and Franklin to talk were obviously high priorities, but she hadn't figured out a way to do it yet. Returning the photo was a matter of keeping her word and had no bearing on the investigation. Following up on the stolen prescription pad and questioning the woman whose name Gwen had given her seemed irrelevant.

But that last one—talking to the woman from the grief group—you might be able to knock that off fairly quickly.

Cassidy had jotted down the name, Ruth Abbot, followed by a phone number. Gwen had told Cassidy that Ruth was glad someone helped her brother die, an attitude Gwen condemned.

Chapter 43

Cassidy found the cordless and dialed Ruth's number. "My name is Cass McCabe. Is this Ruth Abbot?"

"Whatever you're selling, I'm not interested."

"I got your name from Gwen Dickert. She met you in a grief group."

Ruth hesitated. "That must've been the woman who asked for my name and number, then turned her back on me."

"That was her."

"*She,* not her." A pause. "I'm sorry, that's a bad habit of mine. I don't know how many times Ben told me I shouldn't correct people's grammar. My only excuse is that I spent over thirty years teaching high school English." Ruth sounded more amused than contrite.

"That's all right," Cassidy said. "I should be more careful with my pronouns." *In my book, bad manners are worse than bad grammar.*

"So this woman who was not overly articulate passed my name on to you."

"I'm researching an article on euthanasia and I've been interviewing people who had a family member or a friend die that way. Actually, the article isn't so much about euthanasia itself as the impact it has on survivors."

"Are you pro or con when it comes to euthanasia?"

"I'm not taking a stand either way. I want the article to be objective."

"Nobody's really objective. We all have biases that leak through. So what's your personal feeling about euthanasia?"

Not gonna be easy to put anything over on this grammar enthusiast.

"I had a friend who killed herself when her ALS was starting to get bad," Cassidy said. "I'm glad she was able to put an end to her suffering."

"Okay, I'll talk to you."

"Any chance you'd be available this afternoon?"

Ruth chuckled. "I'm retired so my time's pretty much my own. This afternoon would be fine." She gave Cassidy an address in Hinsdale, an affluent suburb about thirty minutes from Oak Park.

Cassidy opened the back door to leave and was dismayed to find Starshine on the stoop waiting to come in. The calico stepped over the threshold and wandered into the interior part of the house.

Shit! You've been working so hard to keep her in.

Yes, but she always gets around you sooner or later.

Cassidy knew exactly how the cat had outwitted her. That morning, before her ten o'clock session, she remembered noticing Starshine hanging out in the kitchen after finishing her breakfast. *Should have realized she was up to something when she didn't go take her morning nap.*

The calico had learned that if she waited patiently next to the door, someone would eventually open it. Which is how she gained her freedom. Cassidy had gone back upstairs, her client came into the waiting room, and Starshine escaped.

Now that she's taken up her old trick again, she might even manage to zip out when you come back from Ruth's. Cassidy decided to shut Starshine in the bedroom.

Cassidy pulled up in front of a white frame residence that looked older and more dilapidated than the imposing houses around it. The woman who opened the door was in her sixties, with long silvery hair held back from her handsome face with a curved tortoise-shell comb.

Cassidy introduced herself.

"Glad to meet you." Ruth gave Cassidy's hand a firm shake. Broad shouldered, almost as tall as Zach, she wore a dark, loose-fitting, ankle-length dress. When she turned around, Cassidy could see that her thick hair extended halfway down her back.

In the living room Cassidy chose a wooden rocker and Ruth sat at a right angle to her in a square cranberry-colored armchair. Fresh air circulated through open windows and the furniture, though far from new, was clean and well kept. Books were piled on the floor and every other horizontal surface. A rotund black cat strolled into the room and plopped onto Ruth's lap.

You weren't exactly impressed when she corrected your grammar but if the cat likes her maybe she's not so bad. Naw, cats are indiscriminate.

"So, let's see," Ruth said. "You want to know the impact on survivors."

Cassidy dug her notepad out of her purse. "That and a lot of other things. First I'd like to hear about your brother and his reason for wanting to die."

"Let me back up and start with my mother's Alzheimer's." Ruth looked down at the cat, her fingers rubbing its neck. "She was an acclaimed anthropologist. When Ben and I were children, she and my father surrounded themselves with some of the most accomplished people in their fields. My brother and I were privileged to sit in and listen to them match wits."

"Those must've been exciting times."

"My father died in his fifties and my mother was diagnosed at sixty-eight. Ben and I should have seen it coming, but we were in denial. We thought that people as mentally active as my mother didn't get Alzheimer's. We made excuses for the lapses we were seeing. We told ourselves it was normal aging." Ruth looked at Cassidy. "Then one day I stopped at my mother's and she was wearing her shirt inside out. When I tried to tell her what was wrong, she didn't understand me."

"Is that when you found out?"

Ruth nodded. Speaking matter of factly, she said, "Ben and I watched our mother slowly disappear. This brilliant, vivacious woman we loved so much became a nonperson."

Cassidy rocked back and forth, her chair creaking. "I've always thought Alzheimer's would be one of the worst ways to go."

"Take my word for it, it is." Ruth waved her hand in front of her face, brushing at the floating cat hair. "When my brother started showing symptoms, we picked up on it right away. That was...let's see...about five years ago."

"You both must've been so scared."

"Not scared exactly. We'd made up our minds we'd never allow ourselves to disintegrate the way our mother had. My brother was a physicist. His whole identity was wrapped up in his intellect. He couldn't bear the thought of losing his mental faculties. Or of having others witness his decline."

"Are you saying he planned to kill himself? But I thought he was euthanized."

Chapter 44

"He initially intended to commit suicide," Ruth said, "but he wanted to keep going as long as he could function reasonably well. His big dilemma was when to do it. He was afraid he'd wait too long and lose the ability to carry out his plan. He asked me to tell him when I thought the time was right, but I refused to take on the responsibility. I didn't want to lose my brother and I was concerned I'd wait too long as well." She wrapped her hand around the cat's tail and slid it from the feline's hindquarters to the tail's wispy tip.

"But he didn't do it alone. He found somebody to help him."

"He did exactly what he was afraid he'd do. He waited until he'd reached the point where he was forgetting all kinds of things and could seldom finish a task. He asked his doctor for help but his doctor wouldn't have any part of it. So of course he asked me." Ruth turned her head to stare out a window. "But I was too selfish. And scared. I couldn't make myself do it."

Cassidy wondered what she would do if Gran made a similar request. "I don't think I could've done it either."

"But he was my brother. He needed me and I let him down. I wasn't as strong as I thought I was."

"So then he found someone else." Cassidy rocked her chair again.

"About two weeks ago he brought me his cat." Ruth smiled and scratched the black cat under its chin. "Einstein here. We'd already agreed that I'd take him when Ben's time came. I tried to get him to tell me what the plan was but he said he couldn't. That he'd promised to keep it a secret. So then I knew he wasn't going to do it himself."

"When did he die?"

"A week ago Sunday."

The day after Gwen's mother? This can't be a coincidence.

"And you know it was euthanasia because he had to keep it a secret?"

"That and the fact that my brother's neighbor saw someone go into his house the night he died. Edna has a balcony overlooking Ben's backyard. She was sitting out there having a smoke at one in the morning and she saw his motion detector light go on. The light was triggered by a person walking toward his stoop. Edna thought it was strange but since Ben opened the door, she assumed there was nothing to worry about."

"Were you the one who found him?"

"He'd asked me to come to his house on Monday. Since he'd given me Einstein the week before, I knew what to expect."

"And then Edna told you about seeing this person?"

"Edna asked if I thought she should notify the police and I told her not to."

Could Paul Goldstein have killed two people? No, Gwen told you Ben had a different doctor.

"Did Edna describe the visitor?"

Frowning, Ruth gave Cassidy a hard stare. "What difference does it make?"

Cassidy shrugged. "No difference. I'm just curious is all."

"The visitor had on one of those hooded sweatshirts so Edna couldn't see the face. Said she wasn't sure of the gender but it looked like a young person."

Cassidy heard the voice in her mind of Claudia's neighbor, Madison Ferris. "A teenaged boy in one of those hoody things." She felt a sudden jolt of surprise and couldn't keep it from showing on her face.

Ruth leaned forward and the cat jumped off her lap. "Do you know who it was?"

"I have no idea. One of the other people I interviewed got a glimpse of the person who euthanized her father and the description was somewhat similar."

"You think it was the same person?"

"It seems unlikely. I can't think of any connection between this person's father and your brother."

Ruth looked like she didn't believe her. "Are you sure you're writing an article?"

"Yes, of course I am. And I really appreciate you telling me about your brother's death."

"*Your* telling me, not *you* telling me. Oh...I'm sorry, I'm doing it again."

Not sorry a bit. It's a game she plays. But I like her anyway.

"Well," Cassidy said, "I guess it's time I asked about the impact of your brother's death on you."

"I miss him terribly. The only person I ever felt closer to was my husband, who died a long time ago."

There was no emotion in Ruth's voice, but Cassidy had no doubt that she felt her brother's loss deeply.

"And at the same time," Ruth continued, "I'm very happy he was able to die the way he wanted to."

Cassidy scribbled down the exact quote, even though she wouldn't be writing any articles.

"Thanks so much for telling me," she said to the older woman.

"Now here's something you can do for me," Ruth responded.   "When you find this person you're looking for—the one who euthanized two people— put him or her in touch with me. I expect to be in need of this person's services a few years from now."

"You have it too?"

Ruth nodded.

Chapter 45

Cassidy arrived at her house fifteen minutes before her next client was due. She went upstairs, grabbed her calendar, then read her email while she waited for the back doorbell to ring.

By the time her session was over, Zach had taken her place at the computer. He said, "Let's go sit in the den and I'll fill you in on Franklin."

They settled in their leather chairs.

"He was at work Monday and Tuesday," Zach said, "so the theory that she dumped him while they were vacationing together is out the window."

"Shoot! That was my favorite scenario."

"But that doesn't mean he didn't kill her."

"How do you know he was at work? I doubt that his boss told you."

"Bosses can't tell you anything so I had to seduce the receptionist to find out."

"You didn't seduce anybody." Cassidy was certain she was the last woman Zach had seduced. *Ninety-nine percent certain, anyway.*

"Here's how I did it." He folded his hands on his chest. "I got a list of the company managers and kept calling until I hit Fred Cantrell's voicemail, which said he was out for the day. So then I went to Franklin's office about an hour before lunchtime and told the receptionist I was there to see Cantrell. She, of course, said he wasn't coming in, and I insisted we had a meeting scheduled and he'd be showing up any minute. So that gave me an excuse to hang around and flirt with her. Which wasn't easy because my flirting skills are pretty rusty."

Don't ask! "What does she look like?"

"Why do you care?"

"I don't. I just want to know."

He grinned. "She has boobs out to here"—he cupped his hands in front of his chest—"small waist and nice tight ass."

"She does not."

"That's what you get for asking. Anyway, I persuaded her to let me buy her lunch. Once we were in the restaurant, I told her I was a journalist investigating a murder and I needed to know whether Franklin had been at work Monday and Tuesday. When we got back to her office, she consulted her computer and told me he had. She seemed to really get off on the idea of leaking info to a reporter."

"We still need to get Franklin to tell us about his relationship with Claudia."

"I think I've got a way in. Remember when I got a police source to describe the crime scene? Well, I went back to that same guy—a dick in Area One—and he was willing to spill some stuff about Franklin. Our best bet would be to pay him another visit and fill him in on what we know."

"You mean now?"

"The sooner the better. I've gotta write an update on the murder or people will forget about it."

"Okay, but I get to drive the Prius."

As they were walking toward the car, which Cassidy had left parked at the curb, she spotted the orange tom sitting in the driveway across the street from their house. "There he is," she said, pointing him out to Zach. "I haven't seen him in so long I was hoping he'd moved on."

She scooted in behind the steering wheel and buckled her seatbelt. "While we're driving, I can catch you up on what I did today." She told him about Ruth and the person wearing the hooded sweatshirt who had euthanized Ruth's brother. "Claudia's neighbor Madison said she saw a teenaged boy in one of those hoody things going in and out of Claudia's house."

Zach thought about it.   "Are you saying you think Claudia euthanized Ruth's brother?"

"Both people were wearing hooded sweatshirts. Madison said it was a teenaged boy.   Ben's neighbor said it looked like a young person.   Gwen's mother was killed on Saturday—the day Claudia supposedly left—and Ruth's brother was killed on Sunday."

Zach shook his head.   "That's about as thin as you can get.   Half the kids in the country wear hoodies."

"You two never quit."   Franklin scowled at them, his feet planted wide, his body blocking the doorway.

"Just wanted to give you a heads up about the story I'm going to write," Zach said.

"Yeah, man, that's the same threat you used last time.   But I haven't seen my name in print yet."

Zach rested his hands on his belt.   "Aren't you going to offer me a drink?"

Cassidy held her breath, wondering if Franklin would let them in.

"Why should I?"

Chapter 46

"So I can tell you what I've got. Then you can decide whether you want to explain yourself or let me write a one-sided story."

Franklin stared at Zach. Cassidy heard children squealing and the blast of a horn. A woman's voice yelled at someone to get out of the street.

Franklin stepped aside so Cassidy and Zach could walk past him. They waited in the living room while Franklin poured drinks. He returned with two glasses of something that smelled like bourbon.

They sat on the same sofas they'd occupied before, a wooden coffee table between them. Franklin took a slug of his drink and said, "So tell me."

"I talked to a cop who's willing to be identified as an anonymous police source. He indicated that a number of texts and phone calls were exchanged between you and Claudia over the last three months. He also told me that some of the emails were sexual in nature and that they often referred to times the two of you spent together."

Hunching his shoulders, Franklin brushed a crumpled sock off the coffee table. "How's giving you more information to use against me going to do me any good?"

"Depends on what you have to say. If I write up what I know about the texts and phone calls, with no comment from you, people are going to think it's pretty strange that you'd get involved with the doctor who caused your wife's death. Some might even suspect that you deliberately got close to her with retaliation in mind—especially since you kept the affair a secret. But if you have an innocent explanation, people are likely to be more sympathetic."

"How do I know you won't slant what I say? Or quote me out of context?"

"I couldn't have kept my job at the *Post* for fifteen years if I did things like that."

Franklin dropped his head and rubbed the back of his neck. "Even though the cops know everything, I was hoping to keep it out of the press. But obviously it's too late for that."

Cassidy asked, "How did you and Claudia come to get involved?"

"I was trying to do the right thing, man." He gazed at the table. "After Randi died, I had an anger problem...Christ, I shouldn't have said that. Well, anyway, I was blowing up at coworkers, my kids...so I went into therapy. Thousands of dollars later, I got over being mad. Like I told you before, I realized that any doctor who'd made the kind of mistake Claudia did had to feel pretty damn bad about it. And that my own actions--following her home and cursing her out--were inexcusable."

He ground to a halt. Cassidy could see he was having a hard time continuing, so she prompted him. "What happened next?"

"My therapist said I should make amends. She wanted me to write a letter but I...I don't know what got into me. I can't explain it, but I felt I needed to do it in person. Maybe I wanted to hear her tell me it was okay, that she forgave me. So I asked her to meet me for dinner and she accepted."

Cassidy and Zach exchanged a look. *So then she vamped him.*

"She was the most—I don't know how to describe her—I just know I'd never felt chemistry like that before. And she acted like she was feeling it too. But I kept telling myself I had to stay away from her. There was no way my kids or family or in-laws would accept my having any contact with the doctor who...."

"But you didn't stay away," Cassidy said.

He traced his pencil mustache with one finger. "When I walked her to her car, she asked if I'd like to get together again, and I said I couldn't. I spent the next three weeks fighting with myself, then I broke down and called her. We met for drinks and I laid out my problem. Said I wanted to see her but we'd have to do it on the sly. I insisted she couldn't tell anybody. Even though our circles didn't cross, I know how rumors get around. I thought for sure she'd laugh in my face but she was fine with it. Surprised the hell out of me."

"What were you planning to do?" Cassidy asked. "Stay in the closet forever? Introduce her to your family at some future date?"

Franklin's eyes drifted toward the window. "Mostly I tried not to think about it."

Like so many of your clients. Jump in head first and don't think about the consequences.

Cassidy asked, "Did you run into any speed bumps? Any issues come up between you?"

Franklin shook his head. "Claudia was so understanding. Whatever happened, she just went with it. I never imagined a relationship could be so easy."

When you know it's going to be over soon, you don't have to deal with anything.

Zach looked up from his notepad. "What about you? Any problems for you? Like her trip, for instance?"

"She said she needed a break. It made sense to me."

"A break from you?" Zach pressed.

"From work. She pushed herself too hard. Put in too many hours."

"When two people are in love," Zach said, "they usually head off for some romantic place together."

"I've got kids. I couldn't get away."

Bet he wanted to go with her but she wouldn't let him. If she actually left town, that is.

Zach said, "You talk on the phone while she was gone? She check in with you every day?"

Franklin looked at the window again.

Zach didn't let up. "She told you she was going to turn off her cell, didn't she? Said she didn't want to have contact with anyone while she was away. And you were pissed about it. Hell, I'd be pissed too. You probably got into a fight. Maybe you even broke up before she left."

"You got it all wrong, man," Franklin said, a snarl in his voice. "We spent the night together before she took off. She needed a break from everything and I was okay with it. We were planning a special night at a hotel in the city after she got back."

Spent the night? Where? Couldn't be his house so it had to be hers. Madison's daughter went over early to help Claudia pack. Suppose it's possible he snuck out before dawn. It was possible, but Cassidy didn't believe him.

"There's one other thing that bothers me," she said. "Claudia told everybody she was going to be gone for a week, but she was shot in her house Tuesday evening. Makes me wonder whether she ever really left."

"That's ridiculous!"   Franklin rubbed his knuckles through the short fringe of hair along the bottom of his chin. "She talked about her vacation for weeks before she went. Why would she say she was going and then not go?"

"Why would she claim to be going for a week and then turn up at her house Tuesday evening? Without telling anybody she was back. Especially without telling you."

"Don't you think I've been laying awake nights asking myself that same question?" He glared at Zach. "This story you're going to write—it'll make me look bad, won't it? You're going to twist what I said and make it sound like I killed her. I was a fool to open my mouth."

Zach scratched the side of his jaw. "All I can do is quote you. You'll probably find it embarrassing to read about your love life in the newspaper, but you didn't say anything incriminating."

Chapter 47

Cassidy pressed a button to start the Prius. She loved being able to turn on the engine without having to dig out her keys.

"I want to stop at Ellen Leavitt's building before we go home," she said to Zach.

"Something we need to find out from her?"

"Something I need to find out. I'd like you to stay in the car." *You connected with her. She probably wouldn't talk if Zach were there.*

"Aren't you going to tell me what this is about?"

"I'd prefer to wait until after I've taken a shot at Ellen. Who's likely to throw me out when she finds out why I'm there."

Zach settled back in his seat and didn't say anything further.

So much more patient than you. Situation were reversed, you'd be having conniptions.

Cassidy struck up a conversation with a group of three older women who were ambling toward the entrance to Ellen's building. The foursome walked past the doorman and into the elevator lobby. Cassidy rode up to Ellen's floor and pressed her doorbell.

Ellen opened her door partway. Her streaked blond hair was mussed and she wore a green terry robe. Her patrician face assumed an annoyed expression. "I don't like being dropped in on."

Cassidy grimaced. "Neither do I. I know it's very rude of me."

"I suppose you're here to nag me about David. Even though I said I'd call, which I did. I left a message on your voicemail about an hour ago."

"Does that mean you've made a decision?"

"As long as you're here, I might as well tell you."
Ellen let Cassidy into the foyer. "When we
discussed David before, you said he was a good kid.
But I had the impression you only talked to him
once. Am I right?"

Cassidy nodded.

"So you don't really know much about him."

"Just what he said." *Plus the fact he had pot on
him and immediately got stoned.*

Ellen patted her hair, apparently trying to
nudge it back into place. "Considering he's been
exposed to Hailey and her boyfriend for the past few
years, he may be more troubled than you realize."

Cassidy braced herself, expecting that Ellen was
going to refuse to subsidize David's lifestyle.

"So before I make a decision," the older woman
continued, "I need to know more about him."

*What's she going to do? Give him a lie detector
test? Hire a P.I.?*

"I need to spend some time with him. Get a
sense of what he's like. I thought I'd agree to put
money in his account for the next three months on
condition that he visit me on a regular basis. If I
like what I see, I'll extend the offer."

*Last time she didn't want anything to do with
him. Today she wants regular visits. Now if David
can only manage not to screw up.*

Cassidy asked, "Would you like me to bring him
the first time?"

"Yes, I think that would be a good way to start."
Ellen took a step toward the door, obviously ready
to usher Cassidy out.

"The reason I came tonight"—Cassidy drew in a
breath—"wasn't about David."

Ellen tilted her head, her face growing wary.

"Could we sit down?" Cassidy turned to face the
living room. "This shouldn't take long."

"I'm not sure..."

"Please?"

"All right."

Cassidy sat in the wingback chair and Ellen perched on the sofa, her back erect.

"I have a question to ask. This may be difficult for you."

"Then stop right now," Ellen snapped. "Whatever it is, just leave it alone. The last time you were here, I tossed and turned all night."

Cassidy's mouth went dry. "First, I want to assure you that anything you say will be completely confidential. I'll tell Zach, but neither of us will breathe a word about it to anyone else." She waited a beat. "Did Claudia help her father die?"

The color drained from Ellen's face. "How can you even think such a thing? She was only eleven."

"If you were sure she didn't do it, you would've said 'no.'"

"What difference does it make? It was almost twenty-five years ago."

"It doesn't, really. I'm just trying to understand her. You may never have talked about this to anyone. But you could tell me and you wouldn't have to worry about it ever getting out."

Ellen twisted her hands together. "I don't know, I don't know."

Cassidy waited.

"Charlie was dying of cancer. He was bedridden and the doctor said it could go on for another couple of months. Just before he died, I got a refill on his Demerol and he begged me to leave the whole bottle of pills on his bedside table. But I was Catholic back then and I didn't want to lose him a day sooner than I had to. And then—two days after he asked me—he died. And the bottle of pills was missing."

"So you knew Claudia gave him the Demerol."

"Not right away.   At first I was overwhelmed with grief.   I couldn't allow myself to believe she might've done it.   I told myself that Charlie would never ask a child to help him, and that the bottle had just gotten lost—that I'd misplaced it.   But later, after the fog cleared, I realized there was only one explanation that made sense."   Ellen looked at Cassidy.   "She never said a word about it and I never asked."

"This has been a big help," Cassidy said.   "And I'm sorry I've stirred up so many bad memories."

"Will you go away now and not come back until you bring David?" Ellen asked, her voice plaintive.

"I won't bother you again until then."

Chapter 48

"She told you that?" Zach said.

Cassidy pulled away from the no parking zone where Zach had waited while she talked to Ellen. "I'm almost as surprised as you. I half expected her to show me the door when I told her what I was there for."

"So why wouldn't you tell me what you were up to?"

"Because you were so skeptical when I said I thought Claudia had euthanized two people. I knew I was on shaky ground with Ellen and I didn't need any sarcastic comments from you before I talked to her."

Cassidy needed to get into the left lane, but the evening traffic was so heavy it took her half a block to find an opening.

"Okay, no wise cracks, but I'm still skeptical. I don't see how the fact that an eleven-year-old Claudia gave her father the pills he wanted makes it any more likely she would've gotten into the mercy-killing business as an adult."

"If we assume Claudia was on a campaign to help people who wanted to die, it explains how she got there. When Claudia handed those pills to her father, I'm sure he was very grateful and made her feel special. She'd been able to do something for him that not even her mother could do. When people exhibit a bizarre pattern as adults, you can almost always trace it back to a significant event in their childhood."

Zach thought about it. "You said she was on a campaign. Does that mean you think her trip was just a ruse so she could hide out at home and euthanize people?"

"Here's where it gets a little fuzzy. I suspect she pretended to drive off Saturday morning and then slipped back into her house sometime during the night. But I don't see why she'd need to hide out for a week or set up this elaborate deception just to euthanize two people. And I have no idea how Ruth's brother managed to contact her."

Zach rested his hands on his knees. "I can feel my skepticism slipping. Even though your theory has some holes in it, when you put it all together it does seem to explain a lot."

"The problem is," Cassidy said, "I don't know where to go with it."

"An even bigger problem is that this would make one hell of a story and there's not much chance it'll ever get written. If Claudia euthanized Paul Goldstein's patient, he had to know about it. But the only way he'd ever tell us anything is off the record."

A problem for Zach but not for you. You don't want that story written. If it showed up in the Post, *Ellen would be certain you'd betrayed her.*

As she started the trek from the garage to the back gate, Cassidy's breath caught at sight of the uneven layers of crimson, orange, and gold hovering above the rooftops in the western sky. She met Zach, who was waiting for her at the gate, and they entered the house together.

Zach went upstairs and Cassidy stopped to use the bathroom next to her office. While washing her hands, she noticed the absence of Starshine. Usually when they'd been gone a few hours, the calico met them at the door, both to greet them and try to wheedle them into an extra meal. *Which Zach often provides when you're not looking.*

Cassidy remembered that Starshine had slipped out earlier and she had shut the calico in the bedroom so she couldn't do it again. Cassidy mounted the stairs, wondering whether she would find the bedroom door open or closed. *Chances are it's open. Zach came home while you were with a client, and holding a thought for hours on end is usually beyond you.*

The door, as she had predicted, was wide open. Knowing it was useless, she looked under her desk, under Zach's desk, under her hanging clothes in the closet, and behind the waterbed. Starshine was clearly somewhere else.

When she got to her feet, Zach was standing in the middle of the room. "Is there any particular reason you're crawling around on the floor?"

"I'm looking for Starshine. She got out this morning so I shut her in the bedroom. But somebody opened the door." She heard the accusatory tone in her voice and realized she wanted to blame Zach. *But since he didn't even know the door was supposed to be closed, there's no way you can make this his fault.*

"She's probably hiding somewhere in the basement," he said. "Punishing you because you locked her up. Open a can of food and she'll come running."

They went down together and she did as he'd suggested. The calico did not appear.

Cassidy looked at Zach. "Any possibility she got out when you came in?"

"I would've seen her."

"I had another client after I got back from Ruth's. Maybe she escaped then." Cassidy grabbed a flashlight out of one of the drawers. "I'm going outside to look for her. And also to see if there's any sign of the demon cat."

Her beam of light probed the densely shadowed base of the garage, the overgrown grass surrounding the lilac tree, the stand of junipers near the stoop. Her flashlight failed to capture any iridescent eyes or small furry bodies.

Cassidy went upstairs where Zach was sitting at the computer. Leaning against the doorjamb, she crossed her arms. "As far as I can tell, there are no cats in the yard. Which doesn't mean Starshine didn't get out. It just means she probably isn't in the yard."

"I searched the main floor and up here. So she must've gone down the basement and won't be seen again until she decides to come up." Whenever Starshine wanted to disappear completely, she headed for their cluttered subterranean level.

Cassidy pictured the enormous orange tom. "I hope you're right."

She took her flashlight, descended the basement stairs, and looked in every hiding place she could think of, with no success. *Doesn't mean she isn't here. The basement has infinite small crannies and you'd never be able to search them all.*

Around midnight, she changed into her nightshirt and went into the bathroom to wash her face and brush her teeth. When she returned, Starshine was curled up on the bed in the space between their heads where she usually spent her nights.

"It's magic. First you disappear, then pouf—you materialize out of nowhere."

Light from the north window brightened the room. Cassidy was sitting up in bed, holding her purple cat mug in both hands, her brain cells gradually blinking on.

Zach came into the room. "I called Goldstein at seven and got his voicemail. No point leaving a message because he's unlikely to call back. In fact, after the way we pressured him into telling us about his affair with Claudia, he's probably going to refuse to talk to us at all."

"I have faith in you. You always find a way to twist people's arms."

Chapter 49

Sitting at her desk, Cassidy reviewed her "Unfinished Business" list. She crossed off the interviewing-Ruth-Abbot and added a new one: "Get Paul Goldstein to tell you about euthanasia." Then she gazed at the next entry: "Find out about stolen prescription pad," trying to remember why she'd put it on the list. Goldstein had told them that his last conversation with Claudia was about a prescription pad which presumably had been stolen by a client. He also said Claudia intended to talk to Jill about it but Jill hadn't received her call. *Can't imagine this has anything to do with the murder. Plus you have no idea how to find out about a stolen prescription pad.*

Cassidy was tempted to ignore it. Then she remembered feeling the same way about her talk with Ruth Abbot, which had yielded a whole new theory about Claudia's activities during the week she was supposed to be gone. *So you probably shouldn't blow this one off.* She realized she could accomplish two tasks at once, return the photo to Jill and pick Jill's brain about prescription pads.

Hey, not bad. Jill's a fun person and you both love dessert.

Cassidy called the clinic and left a message for the nurse. Jill got back to her a short time later.

"I screwed up," Cassidy said. "I promised to get the photo of Claudia and her mystery man back to you right away and I didn't do it."

"Let me call you back."

Cassidy's phone rang in less than a minute. "I went into the bathroom so nobody could hear me. I never did tell Kelly or doctor about finding the purse."

"I hope it's not too late to return the photo."

"After you told me the police already knew about the guy in the picture, it didn't seem to matter. The only other things in the purse were like Kleenex and makeup, so I threw it all away."

"Oh." Cassidy flipped open a catalog that was half buried by the papers on her desk. "I was going to use the photo as an excuse to get together. Over dessert."

"Hey, offer me dessert and I'll follow you anywhere."

"You want to meet at Harvey's?"

"Let's go someplace nicer. My new fave place is The Cake Walk in Wicker Park. It's more upscale and the food's way better."

They agreed to meet at the restaurant at seven that evening.

You're on a roll, sang a gleeful voice in her head. She had taken steps toward accomplishing all but two of the items on her list. The remaining tasks were getting Jordan and Paul Goldstein to talk. She could leave the doctor to Zach, but Jordan belonged to her.

He'd rebuffed her when she called him, but phoning someone who wanted to avoid her was the worst way to go. *Has to be face to face.* She could picture herself standing in front of his condo door but couldn't picture him letting her in. The best approach, she decided, would be to catch him after he finished teaching a class at Columbia College. *He might walk away, but at least he can't slam a door in your face.*

She found his class schedule on the Net. *Well, what do you know? Teaching creative writing from six to eight-thirty tonight. You can head over to Columbia after you've satisfied your sweet tooth with Jill.*

A twentysomething waiter, tall and thin, blond-tipped spiky hair, radiating coolness, whipped around as though on speed. He slowed down, stopped at their table, and gave them his full attention.

"You ladies ready to order?"

Jill chose the apple pie a la mode with caramel sauce. Cassidy went for the brownie sundae with chocolate ice cream, chocolate syrup, whipped cream and nuts. Both opted for decaf to accompany their desserts.

The Cake Walk had an intimate feel to it. Framed collages in pastel colors hung on exposed brick walls and soft jazz played in the background. Cassidy draped her sage green napkin across her lap, propped her elbows on the polished wood table, and leaned forward. "So, how you doing?"

"I'm okay," Jill responded in a listless voice. "It's been tough at work, though. That day we all found out the ten o'clock news had a two-minute segment on the murder, and the next day a bunch of Claudia's patients called to see if the murdered Dr. Leavitt was their Dr. Leavitt." Jill shook her head. "I run into denial all the time but I'm still amazed at how far some people take it. Every one of those patients was hoping I'd tell them it wasn't Claudia."

"I'm forever trying to break through my clients' denial, and then I turn around and catch myself doing it."

Their hipster waiter set plates and cups on the table.

Jill began eating, the blissful look Cassidy had seen before lighting up her face.

Could dessert be the answer to all of life's problems?

Cassidy had eaten just over half of her brownie sundae when her stomach started telling her it couldn't hold another bite.   Trying to ignore it, Cassidy shoveled down two more forkfuls, then laid her utensils on the plate.

"You're not going to leave the rest, are you?"

"I'm stuffed.   You're welcome to finish it if you like."

Jill hesitated.   "No, I'm really full too."

Cassidy said, "Remember when I met you in the parking lot and we talked about the Porsche?"

"Yes."   Jill added more cream to her coffee and stirred slowly.

"Is that your car?"

She raised her eyes, a hint of embarrassment in her face.   "Yeah, it's mine.   I guess I should have told you."

Cassidy waited, hoping Jill would explain.

"You giving me the silent treatment?   I guess that's what shrinks do.   Okay, the reason I didn't tell you is, Claudia gave me such a hard time about buying it, I'm always afraid people will judge me if they know I own a Porsche."

"Why did she give you a hard time?"

"She disapproved of the way I handle money. She lectured me all the time on the virtues of saving.   But me, I'm a life-is-short, dessert-first kind of gal.   I figure, if God wanted people to deny themselves, he wouldn't have created credit cards. So anyway, my uncle left me a small inheritance and I blew it all on a Porsche.   Well, I knew what I was in for.   Claudia acted as if I'd committed a crime because I didn't pay off my credit cards and put the rest into a mutual fund."   Jill watched their waiter dart past them.   "I guess on some level I bought into what she said, because I started not telling people about the Porsche."

"You must've resented all that lecturing."

"Oh, I suppose. But I knew she did it because she cared about me. It feels kind of good to have somebody care enough to get mad when you do stupid things."

Cassidy patted Jill's arm.

Jill moved her empty plate out of the way, deposited Cassidy's plate in front of her, and finished off the soggy brownie.

Crumpling her empty sweetener packet into a tiny ball, Cassidy rolled it between her index finger and thumb as she tried to come up with a good way to frame her next question. *There isn't any good way. No matter how you phrase it, it's going to sound strange.*

Chapter 50

"There's something else I'm curious about. On the night before Claudia left, she found out that one of her prescription pads had been stolen and the thief was writing illegal scripts."

"Yeah, Doctor told me we need to be more careful with them."

"Well, I'd like to know...." Cassidy's gaze was suddenly riveted on a toddler at a nearby table standing on the seat of his highchair about to take a nosedive over the back of it. She jumped to her feet, but before she could do anything, the mother spun around and grabbed the rosy-cheeked little boy.

Cassidy blew out air.

"That was a close call," Jill said.

Settling back in her chair, Cassidy took a moment to get her breathing under control. "What was I saying?"

"Beats me."

"Oh yeah. The prescription pads. Is there any way a doctor would know if one disappeared?"

"Uh uh. The pads get left all over the place. Doctor said he wasn't going to leave them in exam rooms anymore but I keep finding them there. Nobody'd ever notice if one went missing."

"So somebody could've been taking them over a long period of time?"

"I suppose. Claudia had some pretty skuzzy charity patients. One of them could've been stealing pads."

"It could even have been somebody who worked there." *You shouldn't have said that.*

Jill scowled. "Jeeze Louise, what are you saying? You think Kelly or I did it?"

No—you just let your mouth get ahead of your brain.

"Of course not. I meant the people who clean the office. Or anybody else who comes in on a regular basis."

"Are you asking these questions because you think the stolen pad has something to do with Claudia's murder?"

"Not really. I can't see how it could. It's just that I get obsessive. I feel like I have to follow up on every single detail even if it doesn't make sense."

"Obsessive I get. But I don't get why you need to follow up. Or why you're so involved in your husband's investigation. And don't give me that crap about writing a book—I didn't believe it the first time."

Oh shit!

Cassidy laid her napkin on the table, folded it into a neat square, and smoothed out the wrinkles. Looking up, she met Jill's eyes. "I know this sounds strange, but I find Zach's investigations fascinating. He's let me work on a few cases with him before and I get a real rush out of it. When he described the crime scene, it really got my juices going. So I talked him into including me on this one."

Jill looked uncertain for a moment, then said, "I guess everybody's got their quirks."

Cassidy looked at her watch. Eight-fifteen. She was standing in a hall by the door to Jordan's classroom. She had arrived early so she wouldn't miss him if he let his class out before the appointed time. *Which means a fifteen- minute wait with nothing to do. Fifteen interminable slo-mo minutes. And did you mention, with nothing to do.*

Gazing down the hall, she noticed a figure pushing a broom in her direction. *And for entertainment, you can watch a janitor sweep the floor.* As the figure approached, Cassidy could see it was a woman with a red ponytail. When only a few feet away, she stood up straight, put a hand to her lower back, and inhaled deeply. Cassidy was surprised to note that she looked to be in her twenties.

"Back bothering you?" Cassidy asked.

"You talking to me?" The woman glanced around the empty hall. "I usually feel invisible."

"I suppose most people don't talk to...uh...custodians."

"You can call me a janitor. I tell people I work for a temp agency during the day and I'm a janitor at night. Then I make sure they know I'm really a college student saving up so I can pay for my junior year."

"I hope you'll be able to get back to school soon."

The young woman shrugged. "Hard to tell. The costs keep going up. But I'm going to get my degree no matter how long it takes."

"Good for you." Cassidy cupped her right elbow in her left hand. "You don't happen to know if the creative writing class usually gets out on time, do you?"

"No idea. Are you a student?"

Cassidy shook her head. "I'm...a friend of the teacher."

"Dr. Wenzlaff? Seems like a popular guy."

"I suppose half his female students have crushes on him."

The friendly face turned remote. "I should get back to work."

"Wait. There's something you're not telling me."

"I heard some gossip about the professor but I don't really know anything."

"What did you hear?"

"Well, last fall one of his female students was murdered. Right after that, I overheard one teacher telling another that two people who looked like cops went into Wenzlaff's office and escorted him out. The teacher said they took him in for questioning."

"Seems like the police would talk to all the girl's teachers."

"Yeah, I suppose."

"But you think there's more to it."

The woman looked down the hall. "I probably shouldn't tell you this, but everybody was talking about the murder, and I heard some girls say the dead girl told them she was sleeping with your friend."

"Do you think he killed her?"

"It was just gossip and the cops didn't arrest him, so who knows? Look, I gotta get going. I have to finish this building before my shift's over."

Chapter 51

At eight-thirty the door opened and students poured out. When the doorway was clear, Cassidy stepped inside. Jordan stood near his desk on the far side of the room surrounded by a cluster of young women. Girlish voices chattered and giggled, with Jordan's deeper tone undercutting them. As the women drifted away, Cassidy moved toward her former client. She was halfway across the room when his eyes fastened on her, his body going tense. Neither spoke until all the students were gone and Cassidy was standing directly in front of him.

Jordan, looking extremely handsome in a blousy white shirt and tight jeans, put his hands on his hips. "I thought I made it clear. I have nothing to say to you."

"Well," she said in a conciliatory voice, "I have something to say to you, if you'd be willing to listen. I'd like to tell you what Zach and I did after you left my house."

"What difference does it make now?"

"You and I worked together over a long period of time. We have a relationship and that matters to me. I don't want you thinking I betrayed you."

"All right. Go ahead."

She gave him an exact account of the actions she and Zach had taken on the night of the murder.

"So you did call the cops."

"Yes, but we never mentioned your name. I had no idea the police would show up at your place as soon as they did."

He tilted his head one way, then the other, as if weighing his response. "Okay, I believe you."

She allowed an imploring note to creep into her voice. "It would mean a lot to me if you could explain what you did that night."

"So your reporter husband can put it in one of his stories?"

"This will be off the record. He won't be able to use anything you tell me. If he hears the same thing from a different source, he can write about it, but he can't do anything with the information you give me."

Jordan's voice softened. "You want to know why I was in Claudia's house?"

"That's what I keep wondering about."

He stared past Cassidy at some spot on the opposite wall. "I fucked up. I did everything you told me not to."

"After people finish therapy, they often drift back into their old habits."

Jordan met her eyes. For a moment, he looked like the same vulnerable person she'd seen as a client. Then he drew himself up, widened his stance, and hooked his thumbs into his front pockets. His brown eyes turned opaque, his expression unreadable.

Just remembered he can't afford to be completely open with me any more.

"You know how I used to drive by Claudia's house? And you kept telling me not to?"

"You started doing that after she broke up with you, didn't you?"

"Yeah. I did it for a while, but then I was able to stop myself and that was one of the reasons I thought I was ready to quit therapy."

"You started doing it again?"

"Not very often. There's this bar where I know a lot of the regulars, and I'd go hang out there when I had a bad day. Sometimes I'd get a little drunk and then I'd drive by her house, but otherwise I wouldn't." His flat impenetrable eyes looked down into hers. "I stayed away from women for a long time. I just kept going over and over in my head how good it was with Claudia, and how it would never be the same with anyone else. Then I got a little lonely and began seeing someone. She didn't come close to Claudia but it was better than nothing." He stopped talking and gazed at the spot on the opposite wall again.

A couple of seconds passed, then Cassidy prompted, "How did it go with the new girlfriend?"

He looked at Cassidy again. "I thought everything was okay. I was controlling my temper, giving her space. But she dumped me anyway. So the next night, there I was in the bar, remembering all the good times with Claudia. And then I started thinking, if I missed her so much, she must miss me too. I guess I was pretty loaded, because I convinced myself that if I could just talk to her, if I could just get her to see how much I'd changed, she'd take me back."

"So you went to her house?"

"Instead of driving by, I parked and rang her doorbell. When she didn't answer, I took a flashlight out of my glove box and looked in her garage window. Her car was there, so I figured she had to be home, she simply hadn't heard the bell."

"It didn't occur to you she might be out on a date?"

He shook his head. "I was way past thinking rationally. I just felt everything was going to be the way I wanted it to be."

Wishful thinking. Rose-colored glasses. You've done it yourself.

"So then I went around to the back." Turning his head slightly, he looked off toward the corner of the room. "As soon as I realized the house had been broken into, my skin started to crawl. I went into the kitchen...there was this smell...I knew what was coming. She was laying on the rug, completely naked, her eyes staring. I ran outside and puked. I didn't want to go back in but I couldn't leave her like that. Couldn't let anybody else see her all crumpled and naked. So I carried her upstairs and covered her with a sheet. Then I got the hell out."

He turned around, walked to his desk, and perched on its edge. Looking straight at Cassidy, he said, "Are we even now? You told me your story, I told you mine."

She moved closer, reestablishing a conversational distance. "You drove straight to my house after you left Claudia's?"

"I started to go home and then it hit me. The cops would see the order of protection and assume I did it. Then I remembered that session when I told you I wanted to shoot her. I figured those two things together would be enough to make a case against me. There wasn't anything I could do about the order, but I figured you'd always been on my side so I thought you'd be willing to help me." An edge of anger came into his voice. "I never imagined you'd drive such a hard bargain."

Cassidy winced. She hated having him think she'd let him down. *You want all your clients to love you. But you couldn't give him everything he wanted, just like Claudia couldn't, so now you're on his shit list.*

She wrapped one hand around the other and held them in front of her throat. "I'm sorry you feel that way."

"You shouldn't have forced me to sign the fucking consent form."

"So what do you think?" Zach asked. "Was he telling the truth?"   The temperature had shot up that day and they were sitting on their enclosed front porch, sipping a glass of wine as Cassidy debriefed.

"For the life of me, I don't know. I saw a side of him I've never seen before. When I was working with him as a client, he was open, his feelings were right on the surface. Today he was cold and mostly shut down. The only times I could read him were when he said he fucked up, and then later, when he was hostile toward me."

The wind chimes hanging from their eaves made a tinkling musical sound. The air, carrying a faint scent of damp earth, felt soft on her skin. Zach put his arm around her shoulders and she snuggled up against him.

"So you think he might've killed her, then carried her upstairs."

"I believed him up to the point where he said the house had been broken into. That's when he stopped making eye contact. He didn't look at me again until he finished telling me what he'd done while he was in Claudia's house. He could've looked away because he was lying, or because the memory was so disturbing."

An ancient ferry of a sedan, throwing off booming hip hop sound waves, drew up in front of their house. Cassidy gritted her teeth and waited a mind-numbing length of time for the driver to turn off the engine and end the aural assault.

Zach, who'd been rocking to the beat of the music, probably even enjoying it, picked up his wineglass.   "You didn't ask Wenzlaff about the murdered student?"

"I didn't see how I could without making him more pissed off."

"You need a thicker skin."

"I'm perfectly happy being me. I have no desire to be more like you."

"I remember hearing about the case, but it was assigned to another reporter so I don't know any of the details."

Cassidy ran her hand down the arm Zach had draped over her shoulder. "I think I should talk to somebody who knew her. I assume we can Google the murder."

Separating himself from her, he said, "Let's do it."

They found three short articles about the death of Candace Hodge. She disappeared seven months ago on October fifth and was dragged out of the Chicago River two days later with a bullet hole in her chest. She was a sophomore at Columbia College and her mother's name was Maxine Hodge.

Chapter 52

Cassidy sat at a table in the Hyde Park McDonald's where she had arranged to meet David, who hadn't arrived yet. At first she'd thought she would pick him up at a friend's house and save him a trip on public transportation, but then she decided it would be better to spend a few minutes at a neutral place to check him out before they started their trek to Ellen's condo.

Six-thirty and the place was crawling with patrons, the majority of them black. A chaotic mob of people stood in front of the counter. Several older women, probably grandmothers, were trying to ride herd on passels of kids. Single parents were encouraging their progeny to become junk food addicts. Groups of teens yelled at each other and brandished phones.

David came through the glass door and joined her at the table. "Hey, Cass, let's get this show on the road."

"Hey, David, let's take an attitude assessment before we go."

"Oh, so you're going to pre-inspect me before the grandmother inspection."

"Yes." She looked him over. He was wearing baggy jeans identical to the ones he'd had on when she'd seen him earlier. The bulked-up top half of him was clad in a sport shirt, its pocket containing a pack of Camels. His eyes were focused and alert, but she detected a hint of sullenness around his mouth.

Of course he's sullen. How could he not resent being judged by a grandmother who may or may not deign to help him.

"Well, you don't look like you've got any chemicals in your system." She had warned him that if she saw any sign of drug use, she would cancel the meeting.

"I'm not stupid. I want the money."

"You do? Then why so eager to proclaim the fact that you're a smoker?"

He shot her a defiant look. "You said she wanted to get to know me, so I thought I'd be upfront about it. Besides, cigarettes are legal."

"But frowned upon. And not legal for fifteen-year-olds. So you think there's any chance you might be trying to sabotage yourself?"

"Like I said, I want the money."

Expecting Ellen to reject him. Some part of him wanting to take control and give her a reason to do it.

"Have you met Ellen before?" Cassidy asked. "Do you know her?"

"Claudia and I used to go out to dinner with her sometimes, but I don't really know her. She never had much interest in me."

Leaning back in her chair, Cassidy crossed her arms. "You think you could manage to be polite?"

"Yeah, I probably could."

She rose. "All right, let's go."

As they were walking toward the door, she continued. "You've got a lot going for you, you know. You're bright, articulate, and tough. Ellen would be nuts not to want to claim you."

Cassidy, David, and Ellen sat around the rectangular coffee table. Two plates, one laden with brownies, the other with truffles, sat between the outsized chessboard and the colorful glass bird. A dusky light shone through the arched window, and a couple of table lamps cast a yellowish glow.

At first when Ellen opened the door, she'd looked stern and unbending, reminiscent of the wicked headmistresses Cassidy had encountered in some of the books she read as a child. But by the time they were seated, Ellen had managed to curve her mouth into a forced smile. She offered them drinks, then left the room and returned with iced teas for herself and Cassidy, a Coke for David.

Cassidy looked at the boy, who appeared calmer than she felt. *What if Ellen's set the bar so high there's no possibility he could win her approval? God, I hope I'm not putting him through this for nothing.*

The women chatted briefly about the weather. Then Ellen turned to David. "What year are you in school now?"

"Sophomore."

"Have you given any thought to what you'll do after you graduate?"

"Go to college and major in science."

"And how do you expect to pay for it?"

His voice cracked slightly when he spoke. "Claudia said she'd take care of it. Maybe she left me enough in her will."

"If she had a will," Ellen said. "She was so young...."

The room fell silent.

David picked up a brownie and stuffed half of it in his mouth. He chewed and swallowed, then said, "If there isn't any money, I guess I'll have to work and take out loans."

"What are your grades like?"

David looked her straight in the eye. "Not so good. Bs and Cs and a couple Ds. I thought I'd go to a state school my first year and bring up my GPA, then switch to a school like MIT or Cal Tech.

When I went to the Hyde Park School, I was near the top of my class."

Cassidy stared at David, who was wiping his mouth with a napkin. *Actually told the truth about his grades. Expected him to say whatever he thought Ellen wanted to hear.*

"Do you use drugs?" she wanted to know.

David delivered the same forthright look he'd given her before. "Smoke some weed. Not everyday or anything. Don't use any of the hard stuff."

"What about alcohol? How much do you drink?"

The boy continued to meet Ellen's eyes, but the beginning of a frown creased his forehead. "'Bout the same as everybody else. We all party on weekends." He paused. "What about you? How much do you drink?"

Ellen pressed her lips into a thin line. "You know why I'm asking these questions, don't you?"

"Because you might give me money, but only if you decide I'm good enough. I understand it, but I don't much like being grilled."

The self-sabotage part making an appearance.

"I need to know what kind of person you are. Whether I can trust you or not."

"Yeah, but you can't tell anything by asking questions. I could be lying my head off for all you know."

Ellen's shoulders slumped. "So how can I find out about you?"

David shrugged. "Dunno. And by the way, I wasn't lying."

"Is there anything you'd like to ask me?"

"What do you want me to call you? In case I ever see you again."

"Um...you could call me Ellen."

David started tearing a napkin into little pieces, making sure none of them fell on the floor. Then he wrapped the pieces in a second napkin and set it on the coffee table. Staring down at his lap, he asked, "Why didn't you ever come to see me when I was a kid?"

"Oh Lord." Ellen inhaled a deep breath through her mouth. "Because Claudia and I weren't getting along. Because I didn't think I could spend time with you without making peace with my daughter."

Cassidy leaned forward. "It's not too late for you and David."

Should've kept your mouth shut. They need to work this out for themselves.

Another silence.

"How would you feel," Ellen asked, "about coming to see me once a month?"

"I guess that would be okay."

Chapter 53

Cassidy stowed the Prius in the garage and walked along the chain link fence toward the gate. Pushing it open, she went inside her yard and came to an abrupt halt. The orange tom sat facing her midway between the gate and the stoop. He got up on all fours, puffed his fur, and arched his back.

Oh shit! Hair rose on the back of her neck. *This creature looks like it stepped out of a Stephen King novel.*

Now stop that! This is just an overgrown house cat with a massively high testosterone level.

She stared into his large round eyes. "Get out of here. I'm coming through and you're not stopping me."

The tom swished his bushy tail.

Cassidy took two more cautious steps toward the stoop, shortening the distance between her and the cat to about a yard.

The intruder hissed.

Removing her purse from her shoulder, Cassidy swung it around to get the feel of it, then aimed it at the tom's head. The cat jumped from the patio to the grass.

Cassidy moved quickly toward the concrete steps, never taking her eyes off the cat. She went inside the house, then turned to peer through the window in the door. The tom was sitting at the foot of the stairs looking up at her.

At five-twenty the next evening, Cassidy and Zach sat in the Prius in the lot behind the family practice clinic. They'd watched the med tech leave fifteen minutes earlier. The Porsche and the blue sedan sat on the concrete apron, indicating that Goldstein and Jill were still inside.

While they'd been crawling through rush hour traffic, black clouds had accumulated overhead, spewing fat drops that splatted against the windshield. The murky light made it seem much later than it was.

"I'm going to wait by the door to make sure he doesn't get past us," Zach said.

"I'm coming too."

"There's no reason for you to get all wet."

"What's a little rain?" Pulling up the hood on her coat, Cassidy clambered out from behind the wheel. She tried to step across a puddle but it was too wide and one of her good leather pumps landed in the middle. The wind drove rain into her face, stinging her skin and catching in her lashes.

This is stupid. When are you going to get over your adolescent need to prove that anything Zach can do you can do also. Not better, but at least as well. Or almost as well.

They stood with their backs against the wall next to the hinged side of the door, hoping that Goldstein wouldn't see them until he was outside. Several minutes later Jill came out, arm raised to shield her face, and dashed to the Porsche. Cassidy held her breath, fearing they'd be caught in the headlights. The lights blinked on, illuminating the wall on the other side of the door.

She let out a small puff of air. "We got lucky."

"We knew we were taking a gamble—that Jill might see us and warn the doctor."

More time passed, Cassidy's muscles tensing in an effort to ward off the chill from the rain. The door opened partway and Paul Goldstein glanced behind it. Then he pivoted and bolted back inside, slamming the door shut.

Zach pulled at the knob but the door didn't budge.

Cassidy said, "He could go out the front and take a cab, leaving us to stand out here indefinitely."

"Or he could think it over and realize we're going to keep after him until he talks to us."

Cassidy shifted her weight. Her left foot, the one that had stepped into the puddle, felt squishy and cold. She wanted to retreat to the car, but the stubborn part of her that never backed down wouldn't let her.

Eventually the door opened again. The doctor glared at them. When he spoke, his voice was a notch higher than before. "Why are you hounding me? I told you everything I know."

Cassidy slipped around in front of her husband. She said in her soothing therapist voice, "You haven't told us about the euthanasia of Gwen Dickert's mother yet."

Goldstein's head jerked back and his face blanched. "The woman died of natural causes. There's nothing to tell."

"I'm soaking out here," Cassidy said. "Could we please stand just inside the door?"

"Go home and leave me alone. I have nothing to say to you." He started to close the door but Zach blocked it with his foot.

"We'll go off the record again."

"What's the point? What good will it do you if you can't use it in a story?"

"Satisfy our curiosity. We've put a lot of effort into trying to make sense of Claudia's purported trip, and you're the only one who can tell us what she was really up to."

"You're absolutely sure this won't go any further?"

"Cass is a therapist. I'm a reporter. We have a lot of experience in keeping our mouths shut."

Goldstein let out a long sigh and moved back from the door.

Once they were inside, Cassidy pushed back her hood and rubbed her hands together to warm them. She blinked to get the water out of her lashes, then swiped at the strands of hair stuck to the sides of her face.

Paul Goldstein led them down the corridor to his office. Taking the chair behind his uncluttered desk, he held his head in his hands. "You have no idea how hard this is. I promised never to tell anyone."

"You promised Claudia," Cassidy said. "But she's dead."

Not easy for you to break promises either. Even after the person's gone.

Goldstein raised his head and looked at Cassidy. His expression was calmer, as if he'd come to terms with the fact that he was going to have to explain himself. "What do you want to know?"

"It was Claudia who gave Gwen's mother the fatal injection, wasn't it?"

He nodded.

"And then she helped another person die the next day."

"I don't know about that."

"But you do know she'd been committing euthanasia for some time."

He cleared his throat. "Yes."

Chapter 54

Zach asked, "What did she tell you about it?"

The doctor stared into space, a faraway look coming over his face as if he were reliving the conversation. "She first broached the topic quite a while back. She began by feeling me out. Wanted to know what I thought of the Oregon assisted suicide law. I told her I was in favor of it, and then she asked if I'd ever wanted to help a patient die. I said I'd had a couple of terminal patients who'd suffered more than they should have, but I couldn't bring myself to do anything about it." He tapped his pen against his desk. "Then she told me she'd committed euthanasia with some of her patients and if I ever wanted help with one of mine, she'd be happy to provide it."

"That's pretty much what I thought," Cassidy said. "The part I don't get is why she created this elaborate pretense of going on vacation when she never really left."

Goldstein lowered his head again, resting his forehead against his hand. "I shouldn't be telling you this." He was silent for several seconds, then looked up. "Claudia wasn't acting alone. She was part of a small network of doctors who believe terminal patients should have the right to choose the time of their deaths and die with dignity."

Zach let out a low whistle.

"One doctor--they call him the director—started this group a few years ago. The guy's retired now, but he's always tried to maintain a tight rein on things. He established a strict list of rules, but as the network got bigger, there was a tendency for individual doctors to go their own way. So the director set up a series of meetings to get everyone to agree on the rules and pledge to abide by them. This was the first time these doctors had ever met, and since their licenses were on the line, they needed to maintain an even tighter level of security than the CIA."

"You mean the bogus vacation was a cover for Claudia's attendance at these meetings?" Cassidy asked.

"Yeah." Goldstein ran a hand over his bald spot. "If people knew she was in town, she'd be getting calls, her boyfriend would want to see her, the hospital would page her. She didn't want to have to juggle all that."

Zach said, "Were the meetings supposed to last all week?"

"She didn't know how long they'd go on, but she was expecting a lot of disagreement. One of the rules was that euthanasia be restricted to terminal patients—a rule she broke when she euthanized my quadriplegic. She was planning to challenge that one. Another rule she broke was telling me about the network. Everyone was sworn to secrecy, but when we were together...." He sighed again. "Things slip out when you're sharing a bed. Anyway, she figured she could start her trip when the meetings ended."

Cassidy frowned. "The other person she killed—Ben Abbot—how'd she find out about him?"

"When doctors had a patient who wanted to die, they gave the information to the director, and he found a doctor to do it, then reported back to the first doctor so he could make sure he—or--she had an alibi."

Zach cocked his head. "I'm impressed. We put animals down all the time, but it's against the law to provide the same kind of easy death for humans. This director cooked up a brilliant scheme."

You're with Zach all the way on this one.

"The only flaw is," he continued, "when more than one person knows a secret, it eventually gets leaked. I expect Claudia's not the only one who's been guilty of a little pillow talk. Someday this network will get outed, and then I'll have my story."

"I expect you will," the doctor said, his face sagging in defeat. "Can we bring this to an end? You know everything I know now."

"One more question," Cassidy said. "How did Claudia manage to slip in and out of her house without being seen?"

"Let's see...I think she parked her car in the garage that first night, then got herself a rental. Always parked the rental a couple blocks away...set her lights on a timer...dressed like a teenager...."

Cassidy looked at Zach. "I can't think of anything else."

They both stood. "Thanks for your cooperation," Zach said as they turned to leave.

When they reached the door at the end of the corridor, Zach stopped and laid a hand on her arm. "Isn't it about time I got a turn at driving the Prius?"

Tooling around in a rainstorm is about as much fun as shopping in a crowded mall with a blindfold on.

"Well...I guess I could let you chauffeur me home."

Zach put the car in reverse, twisted around to look behind him, and backed out of the parking slot. As he turned out of the alley onto a side street, he said, "Fascinating to hear about the ring of euthanasiasts, but I don't see how it has any bearing on the murder."

"Me either. Someone like Gwen might've felt an urge to do damage to Claudia if they knew she was running around putting people out of their misery, but nobody could have connected Claudia to the deaths."

"So we're back to the enraged lover scenario." Zach squeaked through a light that was turning red. "This pretty much rules Goldstein out as the killer, since they had to have been on good terms for Claudia to tell him about the secret meetings."

"I suppose." Cassidy looked through the rain-smeared windshield at a blur of city lights, dissected by the staccato beat of the wipers. "However, as far as we know, Goldstein was the only one of her exes who knew she'd be at home every night. It's possible he put up a show of good will but was secretly harboring a grudge. Or his lawyer just told him how much he stood to lose in a divorce and he got pissed all over again."

"What is it Shakespeare said? One can smile, and smile, and still be a villain."

Chapter 55

Cassidy didn't make it downstairs the next morning until half an hour after Zach left for work. She refilled her mug, wondering where Starshine was. Zach fed the calico while he waited for the coffee to brew. Then, whenever Cassidy came down, the cat scampered back into the kitchen hoping to score a second breakfast. Cassidy usually held firm, but not always, so Starshine kept trying.

Cassidy remembered watching the calico play with a catnip mouse while she sipped her first mug of coffee in bed. The cat would pick it up by its tail, toss it a few feet, stalk it, then pounce on it and carry it off in her mouth. After that, Starshine had disappeared. *Probably started her morning nap early.*

A bowl of cereal in her hands, Cassidy sat at the dining room table. She had eaten only a few bites when she heard the unmistakable whap of the cat door. *Hey! The cat door's been locked since the first stoop-takeover by the orange tom. At least you thought it was.* She jumped up from the table just in time to see Starshine trotting up from the basement looking pleased with herself.

"What's up? More magic?"

Cassidy went down to inspect the cat door, which Zach had installed in a window above the stairway landing. The door consisted of a plastic flap inside a wooden frame. Beside the flap was a hard-to-turn knob. The knob was set on *closed*, but when Cassidy pushed the flap, it swung outward.

What do you know? After all these years, the damn thing broke.

She went upstairs and shut the door, knowing she would probably forget to keep it closed. When she returned to her breakfast, Starshine was lapping milk from her bowl.

Cassidy finished her eleven o'clock session, then sat at her desk to look through her notes on Candace Hodge, the Columbia College student who'd been murdered.

She called Maxine Hodge, the victim's mother. "My name is Cass McCabe and I'm doing research on three unsolved murders for my dissertation in criminal justice. One of the cases I'd like to study is your daughter's. I know this may be difficult, but I'd really appreciate it if you'd let me come to your house and ask some questions."

"What are you gonna do with the information?"

"Talk to everybody involved and try to determine why the case was never solved."

"I can tell you that right now. The cops did a cover-up. I know who killed her but they wouldn't arrest him."

"I'd like to get the whole story. When would be a good time for me to come and hear what you have to say?"

"I go to work at four. If you can be here by two, we'll have plenty of time." She gave Cassidy her address, then added, "I live upstairs. You'll have to go 'round back to find my bell."

Cassidy drove to Cicero, a low income suburb southeast of Oak Park. The population used to be Eastern European but now was primarily Hispanic. Parts of Cicero were run down, but Maxine Hodge lived in one of the better areas. Tidy brick bungalows with narrow front yards stood on both sides of the street, elbow to elbow like a line of toy soldiers. Cassidy found the address, parked, and circled around to the back door. Next to the door were two bells, the upper one labeled with Maxine's name handwritten on a faded piece of masking tape. Above the door, two porches extended from the house.

Cassidy pressed the bell and a woman leaned over the railing of the second-story porch. "Be right down."

It took a while. Cassidy waited with her arms crossed, soaking up the warmth of sunshine streaming down from a vivid blue sky.

The door opened and a heavyset woman with tired gray eyes said, "You must be Cassidy."

"Hi, Maxine. I'm glad to meet you."

"Call me Maxie. Everybody does."

She was short, with wisps of brown hair straggling around her face. Voluminous sagging breasts above a voluminous round stomach. A colorful tattoo on her fleshy upper arm that said "I heart Candace."

"C'mon," Maxie said. She lumbered upward, using the railing to pull herself along. They crossed the porch and went into the kitchen. Breathing heavily, Maxie plopped down on one of the two chairs that faced each other across a Formica table. Cassidy parked herself on the other.

The ceiling sloped on two sides of the room and the linoleum flooring was so worn she could barely make out the pattern. Behind Maxie stood an ancient porcelain stove, its surface chipped and stained. Cassidy noted that despite the lack of renovation, the place was neat and spotlessly clean.

"So what school are you at?" Maxie asked.

"The U. of I. at Chicago."

"And you're researching unsolved murder cases?"

"I intend to analyze the investigations and see if I can uncover any mistakes that were made."

Maxie gave a cynical laugh. "You think the cops won't cover their asses?"

You do sound naïve. Should've come up with a better story.

"That   could   be   a   problem," Cassidy acknowledged. "But I'm too deep into the research not to continue."

"Whatever." Maxie shrugged.

Chapter 56

"So tell me about your daughter's murder and why the police wouldn't arrest the killer."

"Well, if you're gonna understand this, you need to know that I got pregnant with Candace when I was fifteen and had to drop out of school. And that even though I adored my baby, having a child at that age basically ruined my life. We were so poor, one year we had to live in a hole-in-the-wall place without heat. But after Candace got older, I was able to go to work, and now I have this job as an aide in a nursing home." Turning her head away, Maxie said in a choked voice, "Candace was so excited when we moved into this place."

"Sounds like you had a pretty hard life."

"The reason I told you this is so you'll understand why the two most important things to me were keeping Candace away from boys and making sure she got an education."

"That makes sense."

"I suppose it sounds a little nutty to think I could keep a teenage girl from having sex in this day and age."

"Not to me, it doesn't." *Assuming you could get hold of a chastity belt.*

"But I did it. Candace was a beauty and boys were always buzzing around her, but she didn't want to take the chance of ending up like me. She never dated and didn't go to a lot of parties. Most nights she stayed home and studied so she could get a scholarship. And when she did go out, it was always with her girlfriends." Maxie got to her feet, grabbed a large bag of M & Ms from a cupboard, then lowered herself back onto the chair. She plunked the bag in the middle of the table and ripped it open.

"Help yourself," she said, tossing a handful of M & Ms in her mouth.

Cassidy put half a dozen in her palm and began eating them one at a time. "How did you do it? Get her to stay away from boys, I mean."

"When she was little—maybe six or seven—I started telling her that the reason our life was so crappy was because I got pregnant when I was way too young. That if I'd waited till after college, we could live in a nice house and have a car and most anything else we wanted. And then when she got older, I told her there's only one thing all boys are after and that no matter how nice they seem, you can't ever trust 'em. And you can't trust birth control either. I just drilled those ideas into her head."

Tried her best to turn her daughter into a man-hater. So they could stick together and keep the penis-bearing gender at bay.

"You gave her a clear consistent message and it worked." *At least as far as Maxie knows it did.*

"Everything was going so good. She got enough in scholarships and loans to pay her way at Columbia. Her first year was just perfect. She got good grades, made new friends." Maxie swallowed and her eyes grew moist.

Cassidy put her hand over the other woman's large paw. "What happened?"

"She took a creative writing course."

Cassidy got a sinking feeling in the pit of her stomach.

Maxie grabbed another handful of M and Ms. She crunched on them for a while, then resumed her story. "Jordan Wenzlaff is this handsome asshole professor. He's got all these girls throwing themselves at him, girls who'd be happy to put out. But who does he want? The only girl who isn't chasing after him. That's the one he has to have. So he threatens to flunk her if she doesn't sleep with him, and she's so scared of losing her scholarship she gives in."

"She told you all this?"

"Only after he got her pregnant. That wasn't part of his plan. I guess the rubber had a hole in it."

"Oh my God! That must've been such a shock."

Maxie covered her mouth with her hand. Tears started dribbling down her face and she turned away again. She sat, her shoulders shaking, for at least a minute. Then she got up and left the room. Some time later, she returned and sat down again, her face dry, a wad of toilet paper in her hand.

"If only she'd told me before he started sleeping with her. But he insisted nobody'd believe her. That it was a he said/she said kind of thing. And then when she told him she wouldn't do it anymore, he threatened to hurt me."

"The reason she finally told you was because she was pregnant?"

"She just couldn't handle it all alone any more. Said he'd ordered her to have an abortion but she couldn't bring herself to do it."

"What did you do?"

"I wanted to go right down and tell her dean what that asshole had done to her, but she begged me not to. She said he'd just deny it. But I was going to do it anyway, and then she admitted she was afraid of him. She said he got completely out of control when he was pissed and she didn't know what he might do if we talked to the dean."

A slight shiver ran down Cassidy's arms. *Completely out of control. Sound like anybody you know?*

Maxie continued. "She was so upset I agreed to hold off for a while, and then two days later she went to school...and never came home."

"What a horror story. I can't even begin to imagine what it was like for you."

Maxie looked down at the mottled gray Formica. "They found her body in the river...took me to the morgue to identify her.... Afterward I felt like slashing my wrists."

"When we talked on the phone, you said the police knew who the murderer was but covered it up. What makes you think that?"

"I told the cops everything. My daughter was carrying the asshole's baby. It was obvious he killed her. He wanted her to get an abortion and she refused. But the cops wouldn't arrest him because he was a professor. He had status and money and could afford a high-powered attorney. Candace was a nobody. They weren't interested in finding her killer."

Cassidy opened her mouth to explain that police were always interested in increasing their closure rate and that professors were no big deal, but she stopped herself. *There's no way Maxie's going to let anybody take away her sense of grievance. She's got her grudge and she's going to nurse it till the day she dies.*

Maxie looked at her watch. "I gotta get ready for work, but before you go, would you like to see a picture of my baby?"

"Sure."

Cassidy followed the rotund woman down a hallway to a lace-curtained living room. Maxie went to a tall chest of drawers that held a shrine for her

lost daughter: a fringed strip of white cloth across
the top of the chest; three short narrow candles and
one tall thick one, its wick burning; two trophies;
and a gold-framed eight-by-ten photo of a lovely
young woman in her cap and gown.

"She was so beautiful," Maxie said in a hushed
tone.

"Yes she was." Cassidy felt a lump rise in her
throat.

"I don't know what to think about Maxie's
story." Cassidy bumped her gym shoe against
Zach's on the footstool in the den. "Obviously the
police don't have enough evidence to arrest Jordan,
but that doesn't mean he didn't do it. At first I
thought Candace might've gotten pregnant by
someone else and couldn't face her mother so she
made up a story about her professor threatening
her. But when Maxie said the professor's temper
got out of control, I had to admit it did sound like
Jordan."

Zach folded his hands on his chest. "You're
forgetting the DNA."

"Oh, you're right. Of course the police would've
found out whether Jordan was the father."

"And if he wasn't, I expect they would've told the
mother."

Chapter 57

The sound of banshee howling erupted from somewhere below.

"Oh shit!" Cassidy jumped up and ran toward the stairs. "Starshine got out." She raced down to the first floor, Zach right behind her. They went out the front door and circled around to the side of the house where the cat door was located. Staring at the window with the cat flap in it, she could tell the noise was coming from the basement. She led the way into the kitchen, crossed the room, and started down the basement stairs. She hit the landing just in time to see a bushy orange tail disappear through the cat door.

"Omigod!" Cassidy said. "He must've followed Starshine into the house."

Sucking in air, Cassidy descended to the basement floor. She stood frozen for a moment, afraid of what she might find. Zach went around her and started searching for the calico along the left side of the basement. She walked slowly along the right side, then veered off toward the laundry area.

Starshine sat atop the washing machine grooming one of her hind legs.

Oh thank God!

"Here she is," Cassidy called, rushing forward.

Mwat. Starshine sounded pleased with herself.

Cassidy gazed at a small pool of blood with a tuft of orange fur sticking out of it. "I can't believe it. She must've driven the devil cat off and she's not even half as big as he is."

Zach reached out his hand and the calico sniffed it. He stroked the top of her head, her neck,

and back. "She's not acting like anything hurts."
He held her upside down against his chest, not
allowing her to squirm away.

Cassidy scrutinized the cat's white stomach. "I
don't see a mark on her."

Zach put her back on the washing machine.
She looked like she was going to run away, then
changed her mind and sat up tall, apparently
awaiting further praise.

"She had the home court advantage," Cassidy
said.   "Sort of like when the big muscular
Americans attacked the small Viet Cong in their
jungle."

"Here's hoping the orange tom keeps running
till he's in DuPage county."

Cassidy hoisted Starshine onto her shoulder to
carry her upstairs. "I don't think we have to worry
about keeping her inside any longer."

Cassidy sat on the waterbed, pillows piled
behind her back, Starshine bundled on her chest.
The calico purred riotously, her slitted green eyes
fastened on her human's face.

"You're amazing. Here you are, this petite little
girl, and you vanquished that big bully."

Enveloped in a sense of well-being, Cassidy
delicately scratched the sides of the calico's face.
*Having a cat on your lap who appears to adore you
is even more comforting than a bag of peanut butter
cups. It puts things in perspective. You may never
know whether Jordan killed Claudia or the student,
but it really doesn't matter as long as Zach and
Starshine are safe.*

The phone rang. Cassidy couldn't reach the
cordless on her nightstand so she didn't answer.
She thought Zach would pick up in the computer
room.

He appeared in the doorway. "It's Jill."

"Can you hand me the phone?" Cassidy pointed her chin toward the cordless, which sat between a paperback book and a box of tissues.

He gave it to her and she maneuvered to get it to her ear without moving any part of her body occupied by Starshine. The smallest disruption usually caused the cat to depart.

"Hi Jill. What's up?"

"I was visiting a friend in Oak Park and she wanted to know all about Claudia's murder. And I spent almost an hour talking about it."   Jill sounded as though she were on the verge of tears.

"Where are you now?"

"In my car. Just sitting here, not moving. As soon as I left her house, this horrible black cloud wrapped itself around me."

"Um...so is there anything I can do to help?" Cassidy's free hand scratched behind Starshine's ear.

"Those other times we talked, I always felt better afterward. But I shouldn't even be asking. That's what you do for a living."

"I wouldn't mind spending some time on the phone with you."   *Especially if Starshine stays planted on my lap.*

"Actually, what I'd really like is some face time. But I don't expect free therapy. I'd be happy to pay for a session, even though I'd probably only need fifteen or twenty minutes."

Shit. That means you'd have to get up, change clothes, get your head into work mode.

"Well, I guess that would be okay. My house is on the southwest corner of Hazel and Briar. Come to my back door, ring the bell, then come inside and wait in one of those wicker chairs. It's going to take me a few minutes to get ready."

"You don't have to dress up or anything."
"Trust me, I do."

Chapter 58

Cassidy poked her head into the computer room and told Zach that Jill was on her way over. Hurrying downstairs, she unlocked the back door and turned on the lights, then returned to the bedroom. She threw off a stained sweatshirt and an old pair of floppy jeans, clothes she wore only when she was sure no one but Zach would see her. She grabbed a pair of black knit pants and reached for a blouse, then considered the cool temperature and put on a sweater instead.

She was about to go searching in the back of her closet for her heels when the doorbell rang. *Just wear your gym shoes. You're not required to be totally professional for a drop-in.*

She ducked into the bathroom to pull a comb through her hair and sighed over her lack of makeup, then went downstairs. Stepping through the doorway into the kitchen, she spotted Jill at the far end of the room leaning against a small counter next to the office door. She wore a brown coat and was dabbing at her nose with a tissue.

"Hi," Cassidy said, crossing the kitchen toward her.

"It's really nice of you to let me come over on such short notice."

Cassidy paused. Jill's voice sounded matter of fact, no tinge of sadness at all. *Must be feeling better now that she's here.*

Jill moved sideways so that her back was to the office door, giving Cassidy more space to go around the room divider into the waiting room.

"Would you like a cup of..."

Cassidy heard a noise behind her. She spun, seeing for the first time a man who'd been standing

with his back against the room divider. Medium
height, broad shoulders, a black handle-bar
mustache. She knew she'd seen him before but
couldn't remember where. Every muscle in her
body tensed.

"Who are you?"

Jill grabbed her, one hand covering her mouth,
the other clamping around her stomach so she
couldn't break away. Cassidy's heart pounded and
her skin went cold. She tried to scream but Jill's
hand tamped her voice down to a whisper. She
grabbed Jill's hand and tried to pull it away from
her face but it didn't budge. She raised her feet off
the floor and let herself drop, hoping the weight of
her body would break Jill's hold, but the nurse's
hand never wavered.

Finally she thrust her jaw forward and bit Jill's
palm.

"Ow!" Jill held Cassidy tighter. "You little shit.
Do that again and I'll knock you out."

Cassidy stopped fighting and focused on the
man, who'd just ripped a few inches of duct tape off
the roll he was holding. Jill removed her hand and
before Cassidy could inhale enough air to scream,
the man stretched the tape across her lips.

*Oh God, they're going to kill you. And Zach too.
You can't even warn him.*

Jill pressed something cold and hard against
Cassidy's temple. "You know what this is?"

Cassidy nodded.

"Lie face down on the floor with your hands
behind you." Jill's voice was pleasant, almost
friendly.

*You could let them shoot you and Zach would
hear it and know something's wrong.* But before
she finished the thought, her knees buckled and
she lowered herself to the floor.

The man's hands, rougher than Jill's, crossed her wrists and held them together while Jill wrapped tape around them. When they were secured, Jill helped Cassidy to her feet.

"We're going out to the car," Jill said.

The man shoved the barrel of a large gun into the small of Cassidy's back and marched her out the door, Jill falling in behind him. As they walked toward the gate, Cassidy looked at the SUV parked at the curb. *Not Jill's Porsche, not the cops-are-pigs sedan. Probably stolen.*

Jill opened the back seat door and climbed into the SUV. "Okay, you next," she said to Cassidy. Cassidy hesitated, but the man prodded her with his gun and she scrambled inside. He slammed the door behind her.

Cassidy's gaze zoomed in on the small ladylike gun Jill now held in one hand.

"Don't worry, I'm not going to shoot you just yet. I know how curious you are, so I recommend you watch out the window and see what comes next. Earl just went back into your house."

Earl...where did I hear that name? She pictured a label bearing the name "Earl Grapski" above a door buzzer. *Hailey's really tough, really mean boyfriend.*

As Cassidy stared at the stoop, she heard Jill shuffling around. She turned to see that Jill was holding her gun in her right hand, her cell in her left.

She said, "This is Jill. Cass is sitting in the car right next to me. Her hands and mouth are taped and I have a twenty-two aimed at her head. If you follow my instructions exactly, I won't pull the trigger. I want you to stay on the phone and keep talking—doesn't matter what you say—and get your butt down to the waiting room in the next thirty seconds. If you don't, the next sound you hear will be my gun firing."

Cassidy picked up the faint sound of Zach's voice: "La, la, la..."

Her stomach lurched.

Nearly a minute passed before Jill spoke again. "Earl says he's got Zach's hands and mouth taped and they're coming out." She put her phone in her coat pocket.

Cassidy twisted back toward the window just in time to see Zach come out with Earl close behind him. He deposited her husband in the passenger seat, then climbed behind the wheel and started driving.

Swiveling his head, Zach met her eyes and she could read his thought: Somehow we'll get through this.

"Oh you lovebirds. You're just too cute," Jill said. Then, dropping the sarcasm, she continued. "You know, Cass, I never wanted this to happen. I *liked* you. Even thought we might be friends. But you couldn't leave anything alone. You had to pick, pick, pick. When you said somebody at the clinic might be stealing prescription pads, I knew you had to go."

Omigod! Never occurred to you that Jill was the thief. She stole the pads, Earl peddled the scripts.

The SUV went south on Austin Boulevard and Jill turned away to look out the window. Cassidy was relieved. She intended to work on freeing her hands, and to do so she had to move her shoulders. If Jill were watching, she'd realize what Cassidy was up to. She began twisting her wrists. Initially, she could barely move them, but if the drive was long enough she thought she could loosen the tape sufficiently to slip her small hands out. She noticed that Zach had turned toward Earl and that his shoulders were moving also. *Of course he's doing the same thing you are. But his hands are so much bigger it'll be harder for him.*

Earl cruised down the entrance ramp onto the Eisenhower Expressway and headed west. It was a Sunday night, around nine o'clock, and the traffic was light. *For once, you'd prefer gridlock.* A short time later they switched to I-88, a tollway that went directly west out into the boondocks. By the time they reached Aurora, a town that lay almost an hour's distance from the city, Cassidy had loosened the tape enough that she was certain she could free her hands when she wanted to.

Several miles past Aurora, Cassidy noticed a change in the landscape. They had left suburbia and were surrounded by farmland, flat and empty except for occasional houses, barns, and trees. Turning left onto a gravel road, Earl drove past a lighted farmhouse. He continued a few miles farther and turned right, then right again, into a long driveway. The ghostly light from a nearly full moon enabled Cassidy to see the two-story house ahead of them. The front door stood open, the window to the left of the door had a jagged hole in it, and a drainpipe dangled from the corner of the roof.

Earl steered the SUV over dried grass toward the rear of the house. They drove around a one-story addition that looked as if it had been cobbled onto the side of the original structure. Earl stopped near a large back porch covered by a gently sloping roof. Spiky evergreen bushes clustered on both sides of the porch, leaving only a narrow path to the steps.

Hopping out of the driver's seat, Earl switched on a flashlight, then dragged Zach and Cassidy out of the car. Joining them, Jill stepped close to

Cassidy and put her pistol to Cassidy's head. They all followed Earl as he went to the rear of the car.

Shoving his flashlight into his jacket pocket, Earl said to Jill, "Don't let them get too far apart."

"I know what I'm doing. Zach isn't going to try anything as long as Cass's life is on the line."

Earl shot Jill a skeptical look. "You think he's willing to die for her?" He barked out a gravelly laugh, then took two gas cans out of the SUV.

Fear sucked the air out of Cassidy's lungs. The thought of being burned alive terrified her.

Please, oh please, let them shoot us first!

Chapter 59

Earl tromped along the path between the bushes and into the house. Jill took a step back, held her gun in both hands, and pointed it at Cassidy.

"You go first, Zach."

He started toward the house, with Cassidy behind him and Jill bringing up the rear. As they neared the back door, Cassidy picked up the smell of gas. Inside the kitchen, the fumes were so strong she began taking short shallow breathes.

Moonlight from the windows made it possible for Cassidy to see where she was going. Old newspapers, plastic bags, beer cans and other debris littered the floor. A wooden chair lay on its side. A two-legged table tilted against the wall.

"Go down that hall," Jill instructed. She turned on a flashlight and directed the beam toward a dark corridor at the opposite end of the kitchen.

Cassidy glanced behind her. Jill had the flashlight in her right hand, the gun, hanging at her side, in her left.

"Turn your head around and don't look back," Jill said sharply.

They traversed a long corridor, passing open doorways off to either side, a cramped stairwell in the middle. When they reached the end, Jill herded them into the living room, where Earl was pouring gas on the floor. Cassidy jerked back away from the overpowering fumes. She felt a gun barrel prod the back of her head. Her blood running cold, she took a step forward, stopping near Zach.

The nurse remained just inside the hall. "Let's do them now so I can get out of here."

"I'll take care of it." Setting down his gas can, Earl took out his flashlight and gun. He aimed the gun at Zach. "Go back down that hall and up the stairs."

"What? Why take them upstairs?"

"Can't shoot 'em down here. Too much gas."

Carefully enunciating each word, Jill responded, "Then you should have killed them first."

"Shut your yap." Earl shoved his gun into Zach's chest.

"You've got it all wrong," Jill yelled. "You have to keep the gun on Cass. That's the only way you can be sure of controlling Zach."

"He's not gonna do anything while I've got this Glock on him."

"Just do what I say!" Jill demanded.

"Fuckin' bitch," Earl grumbled under his breath. "You, Zach, get in front of your woman."

Cassidy could see by the worried lines on Zach's forehead just how much he didn't want her to take his place in front of Earl's gun.

With Earl lighting the way, they marched to the stairwell. He pointed his beam up the stairs and Zach raced toward the landing. Cassidy ran after him. As soon as both feet were on a level plane, she spun around. Earl was running also, four steps behind her. She raised her foot and smashed her gym shoe into his face. His arms flailing, he went over backward.

"Sonuvabitch!" His head landed with a thud near the bottom of the stairs. The flashlight went flying out of his hand but continued to shine from somewhere on the floor.

Cassidy stood frozen, waiting to see if he'd pick himself up. Jill appeared in the frame. She fired off a shot at Cassidy, who went stumbling around the corner out of their sight.

She listened for Jill's footsteps on the stairs. Instead, she heard Jill speak to Earl.

"Can you hear me?"

He moaned.

Now in complete darkness, Cassidy realized she would need her hands to guide her. So she tugged at the tape around her wrists until one hand slipped free.

"Can you hear me?" Jill said again in a louder voice.

Cassidy ripped the tape off her mouth, wincing as the tape tore at her lips.

She ran her right hand against the wall and began climbing the second flight of stairs. A muffled noise came from the hall above. She looked up and saw Zach standing in an area where a dim light was filtering in. Climbing farther, she discovered that the light was coming from a large hole in the roof above the hall.

She removed the tape from his mouth, then threw her arms around his broad chest.

"I heard a shot," Zach said, "and when I looked behind me you weren't there."

"I kicked Earl downstairs and then Jill fired at me. I got myself out of sight but I could hear her trying to rouse Earl. He seemed to be injured, but I have no idea how badly. And even if he's out of the game, Jill's likely to come after us."

They stood listening. Cassidy could hear a male and female voice, but it didn't sound as if they'd started up the stairs. "I guess Earl's recovering. God, I hope they don't decide to torch the place."

"Even if they do, we still have a good chance of making it out." Zach drew in a deep breath. "Get the box cutter out of my jeans pocket and cut the tape off my wrists, will you?"

She retrieved it and sliced the tape. "Where'd you get a box cutter?"

"Grabbed it on my way out of the house."

"We need to check all these rooms, see if there's a way out."

"You take the ones on the right." Zach trotted toward a doorway on the left.

Cassidy went into the nearest room on her side, a corner room, furnished with a single bed frame minus its mattress, a small chest of drawers, and a vanity with a cracked mirror on top. She tried to open one of the windows but it wouldn't budge. When she looked down at the ground, her chest constricted and goosebumps rose on her arms. *No way you'd ever be able to make yourself jump from this high up.*

Chapter 60

The next room was a corner room also. It had a double bed, newspapers scattered across the top, and a massive dark wood chest of drawers that stood against the wall to her right. One of the windows was halfway open. Two feet beneath the window a wide porch roof extended from the house. She could see the SUV, so she knew the roof was covering the back door. She felt certain she could make her way to the edge of the roof and lower herself to the ground from there. She strained to push the window upward. Creaking, it moved another inch. *This is it! The way out.* She went running to find Zach.

"I think I heard footsteps," Zach said when they were both in the room. "We've got to get that chest against the door."

Cassidy and Zach each took one side and tried to drag it away from the wall. Zach moved his side out about a foot. Cassidy was able to move hers only a few inches. Zach worked on her side and got it out the same distance as his. They leaned their shoulders against it and scraped it into position in front of the door.

Sweat beaded her forehead and her legs were weak. Breathing heavily, she propped her back against the wall. Zach was down on one knee across from her, examining something she couldn't see.

She heard Earl's gravelly voice. "The room with the closed door."

Cassidy stared at the chest. *It'll stop them. It has to.*

The doorknob rattled. A thud sounded, then another. She pictured Earl slamming his foot against the door.

The crack of a gunshot, its blast reverberating inside Cassidy's skull. She clapped her hands over her ears. Several more shots, and then a body hitting the door.

"Fuckin' assholes!" Earl shouted. "You don't wanna die the easy way, then burn, baby, burn!"

Cassidy's mouth went dry. She couldn't understand why Zach was still on the floor. *We should be climbing out the window right now!* She looked over his shoulder and saw that he was removing a metal grate from the floor.

"What are you doing?" Her voice shrill.

He stood and began grabbing up newspapers from the bed. "There aren't any ducts. You can throw something straight down to the floor below."

"We haven't got time!" She yanked on his arm.

He looked her in the eye. Spoke slowly and deliberately. "Climb out that window, jump off the roof, and get as far away as you can."

Cassidy suddenly realized what he was planning to do. Fear gathered deep in her belly. "No, don't!"

He continued to look straight at her. "We're both going to get out of here alive. Now do what I said."

Reluctantly she raised the window all the way and climbed out onto the roof. She crept to the edge and looked down. The thick bank of evergreen bushes would break her fall. She took a deep breath, then turned to look at Zach.

He was on the roof, one knee braced against the windowsill, his upper body leaning inside the window. He held a ball of burning newspaper.

Cassidy's heart skipped a beat. *He'll never make it.* Instinctively she took a step toward him.

He lobbed the wad of paper into the room, then instantly pulled himself out of the window, moved sideways, and flattened his body against the wall.

A deafening explosion.   A shower of broken glass. A blast of hot air that lifted her off the roof and dropped her into the bushes.

She landed face up, then slid to the ground, branches scraping her skin and ripping her clothes. She was dazed and only partially conscious. Smoke stung her nostrils. Sharp pieces of gravel jabbed the back of her head. Her eyes itched.

As she struggled to sit up, every muscle in her body ached. She stared at flames shooting out of the ground floor windows, her mind gradually clearing.

Zach! Where is he? She picked herself up and took a few wobbly steps. An eerie orange light lit up the whole area. She sucked in hot air. *Gotta find Zach.* Forcing herself to put one foot in front of the other, she started to regain her strength.

A woman screamed. Jill, flames licking at her coat and hair, came racing around the corner. Cassidy hesitated. *You touch her, you'll get burned.* Then, on a burst of adrenaline, half stumbling, half running, she went after Jill, closing the distance quickly because of Jill's erratic course.

With only a couple of feet between them, Cassidy threw herself at the taller woman. Jill hit the ground, Cassidy on top of her. Screeching even louder, kicking and flailing, Jill tried to push Cassidy away, but she managed to roll Jill over until the flames on her coat were extinguished. Kneeling over Jill, Cassidy could see her hair was still on fire.

Zach appeared as if from nowhere, hauling off his tee shirt and wrapping it around Jill's hair. When the flames were out, he helped Cassidy to her feet.   Her eyes watered from the smoke.   She started to wipe them, then realized her hands were covered with dirt.

"I can hardly see."

"Me too."   Zach pulled a reasonably clean handkerchief from his jeans pocket and gave it to her. She dried her eyes, then returned it to him so he could wipe his eyes also.

They looked down at Jill. She lay on her side, her face burned, her arms and legs pulled close to her body. "Help me," she implored in a faint voice.

"Blankets," Cassidy said and started walking unsteadily toward the SUV. Glowing cinders drifted in the air around her. She and Zach searched the vehicle but found nothing they could use to cover Jill. They also didn't find a key in the ignition.

They went back to see how Jill was doing. She appeared to be unconscious. Cassidy called her name and got no response.

Facing away from the house, she felt intense heat at her back, although the front of her body remained cool.   Zach experienced a spasm of coughing. They agreed they shouldn't move Jill. Cassidy felt she ought to stay with her, but Zach convinced her there was nothing she could do.

They huddled together on the bench seat in the rear of the SUV. Huge orange and yellow flames enveloped the house and rose high in the sky like a beacon. The air inside the car was stifling.

Cassidy said, her voice croaky, "I can't stand to think she might be dying out there."

"If she is, she brought it on herself."

"I suppose Earl took your cell phone."

"Yeah."

"Mine's on my desk in the bedroom."

Zach put his hand on her knee. "It shouldn't be too long before somebody sees the fire and comes to check on it. The police or a volunteer fire department."

"I guess Earl must be dead. Or at least in bad shape. Otherwise he would've shown up by now."

"You're probably right, but it wouldn't hurt for me to walk around and see if I can spot him." Zach got out of the car and started circling the house. Before long he was back in the SUV. "No sign of him. Probably didn't make it out of the house."

Despite the heat, Cassidy snuggled up against her husband's bare chest. "I couldn't see you anywhere. I was so afraid you'd died in the blast."

"I stepped off to the side of the window because I knew those gas fumes would go off like a bomb. You were standing right in front of it and I saw you go sailing off the roof. Then I jumped into the bushes. Must've hit my head on something 'cause I blacked out for a while. I came to a couple of minutes before I heard Jill screaming."

"Why did you start that fire? It would've been so much safer just to get away before the house went up."

He shook his head. "I wanted to get rid of Jill and Earl. If we'd jumped off the roof and they'd come out with guns in their hands, they could've hunted us down. There's no place to hide and with all this open farmland, we couldn't have gotten away."

They were quiet for a couple of beats. Then Zach picked up her hand and gently rubbed his fingertips over her palm. "I can feel the burned skin."

"I know they're going to hurt later, but I can't feel anything yet."

After what seemed a long time, a number of shrieking police cars pulled into the driveway.

Chapter 61

Standing just outside the door to Jill's condo, Cassidy felt her jaw clench.

This woman tried to kill you and Zach. You can barely stand the sight of her.

Yes, but if you don't at least pretend to be nice, you'll never get the answers you want.

Cassidy opened the door and let herself in. When she'd arranged the visit, Jill said she'd leave the door unlocked because it was painful for her to get up and down.

"Hi Jill." Cassidy crossed the room, a small white box in her hand. "I brought you some cheesecake."

"Is it poisoned?" The nurse was lounging amidst a nest of pillows on the loveseat.

"Why would I take a chance like that when I can just sit back and let the state's attorney do his job?"

"You have a point."

"Would you like me to take this into the kitchen and put it on a plate so you can eat it now?"

"No thanks." The nurse wore a filmy silk robe, exotic flowers splashed across a white background, with an elegant turban covering her head. Her face was red and shiny, and her eyebrows were gone.

Three weeks after the fire, Jill was recuperating in her condo instead of Cook County Jail, thanks to the good fortune of being brought before a judge who granted her bail.

"I'm glad you were willing to see me." Cassidy, sitting in a lightweight contemporary chair at a right angle to the loveseat, put the box on a glass coffee table.

"Well, you did save my life. Besides, I told you before I like you...and I can use the company.

Seems like none of my friends is willing to admit they know me since I had my two minutes of fame on TV."

"So how is your case looking?"

"Jeeze, I really screwed myself, you know? I can't believe I said what I did."

"You mean when you confessed in front of the cops?"

"That was so stupid. If I'd only kept my mouth shut, I could've said it was Earl who killed Claudia. But me, I have to be a blabbermouth to the end."

"I thought you did it because you believed you were dying."

"That's no reason. You don't suppose I have a conscience, do you? If I do, it's never gotten in my way before. You know what my lawyer said? If I'd blurted it out while the cops were questioning me, it wouldn't have been admissible because they hadn't read me my rights. But me, I had to say it before they asked me anything, so it's considered voluntary." Her red face twisted into a scowl. "Nothing ever goes my way."

I'd say everything was going her way before she tried to kill us.

Cassidy asked, "Would you mind telling me about Claudia's murder?"

"More questions. I never met anybody as nosy as you." She gave Cassidy an appraising look. "Are you here as a spy for Zach? Or a therapist who can guarantee confidentiality?"

"I can't not tell Zach. But I can promise that anything you say will be both off the record and privileged."

Jill tilted her head one way, then the other, causing her turban to slip sideways. She straightened it with her bandaged hands. "Oh, why not? I know you'll keep your promise. You're so nauseatingly sincere and principled it's almost leaking from your pores."

"To start with, I'd like to know why you did it."

"Claudia figured out it was me who stole the prescription pad and I knew she'd turn me in. I could've gone to jail. At the very least, I would've lost my license."

"How did she know it was you?"

"Back when we were living together—when I was going to nursing school—she caught me with a stolen pad. I vowed never to do it again and she forgot about it. Then that night when she stayed late and got the call from the pharmacist, she assumed at first that the pad'd been taken by a patient. She called me and said we all had to be more careful. Then she called again twenty minutes later and said she'd just remembered the pad I'd stolen before and that she was going to have to talk to me about it when she got back from her trip."

"Did you have any reason to think she wasn't really going to leave town?"

Jill shook her head.

"So what made you think she'd be at home that Tuesday night?"

"Well, as soon as I realized she suspected me of stealing the pad, I knew I had to kill her."

Cassidy felt chilled. *Talk about cold-blooded.*

"So I called Earl and told him to follow her. My first thought was that I'd shoot her in some motel room and everybody'd think it was a robbery gone bad. That's why Earl got a silencer. But then he discovered she was coming home every night."

"So you went to her house and shot her?"

"Earl helped me break in and then he left. I was waiting for her when she got home. I made her throw her clothes around the room so it'd look like one of her lovers killed her. And it worked. The cops hardly even questioned me."

Cassidy pictured the dark figure firing at her in her neighbors' yard. "Why you instead of Earl? I got the impression he was more experienced at shooting people."

Jill's red face suddenly changed, her amiable expression shifting to one of bitter resentment. "Because I *wanted* to. Because I was sick of her superior attitude. She was the doctor, I was the nurse. She had men falling all over her, I didn't even have a boyfriend. And she was forever telling me I shouldn't spend money, shouldn't eat sweets, shouldn't waste time shopping. Everybody thought she was so wonderful, but she destroyed Doctor's marriage and fucked over every man who ever cared about her."

"You must've hated her."

Jill breathed out a long exhalation ending in a sigh. "Yeah, I did. Or at least a part of me did. But there was some part of me that loved her. After she was dead, I was surprised as hell at how much I missed her." Jill looked down at her bandaged hands.

A moment of silence. Cassidy glanced around the sleekly designed living room. Pale apricot walls with a cherrywood coffee table. Darker apricot furniture, a loveseat and easy chairs. A huge abstract painting in bold colors above the loveseat.

Expensive clothes. Expensive condo. A Porsche. Prescription drugs must sell for more on the street than I ever would've guessed.

Cassidy said, "I suppose you wrote out the scripts and Earl sold them."

"Yeah."

"But wasn't that risky? Pharmacists call doctors all the time to verify prescriptions."

"Doctors never answer the phone. I paid Kelly a small sum to give me all the message slips from pharmacists to Claudia and then I returned the calls posing as her. Kelly probably guessed what I was up to but we never talked about it."

Cassidy cupped her hands in her lap. "There's one other thing. Evidently you told Earl to watch my house and kill me. But I have no idea why you wanted me dead before I said a thing to you about the prescription pad. It never occurred to me that either you or Earl was involved in the murder."

"That was dumb ass Earl acting on his own. In fact we had a big fight about it when I found out. He Googled you and Zach and discovered you were a social worker. So then he started worrying that you'd report Hailey's drug use to DCFS and she'd lose custody again. And if that happened, Earl wouldn't have been able to get his hands on David's inheritance."

"Do you know how much Claudia left him?"

"I'm the executor of her estate, so of course I do. And—as you'd expect—David's the sole beneficiary. When I needed Earl's help in planning the murder, I told him how much David stood to inherit. What I didn't tell him is that the money's set aside for college. But I didn't need any carrots to use on Earl, since if I'd gone down for selling scripts, he would've gone with me."

"Weren't you afraid of what Earl would do when he found out he couldn't steal David's inheritance?"

Jill shrugged. "Not really. I planned to start signing Doctor G's name on the scripts and Earl wouldn't have wanted to cut off his revenue stream."

"So the reason I became a target was Earl's fear that I might report Hailey."

"Yup."

Cassidy looked at her watch. "I've gotta get going. I have a client this afternoon."

Disappointment clouded Jill's face. "Will you come back and visit me again?"

Unbelievable. First she tries to kill you, then she wants you to be her friend.

But she's so lonely, the sappy part of Cassidy said.

And she deserves to be!

Cassidy met Jill's eyes. "I'm sorry, but I won't be coming back. Before I go, would you like me to put this cheesecake on a plate?"

Jill's face brightened. "Yes, thank you, I would."

Cassidy took the box into the kitchen, prepared the cheesecake to be eaten, and handed it to Jill.

Chapter 62

A few days later Cassidy was tearing off pieces of lettuce and arranging them in two salad bowls when Zach came home from work. At her feet Starshine was playing with a lettuce leaf she'd stolen from the counter.

"Hey," he said.

She turned to face him. "Hey, yourself."

Zach stood in the middle of the room, his hands on his belt. "That Columbia College student who was murdered? You'll be happy to know Jordan didn't do it."

"That's wonderful. How'd you find out?"

"I tracked down one of the dicks assigned to the case. Since there's almost no chance they'll ever be able to close it, he was willing to talk to me. Turns out the father of the baby was a lowlife punk who lived next door. That girl—what was her name?"

"Candace."

"Her best friend told the cops that Candace's mother couldn't stand the punk, whose street name was Luv Dawg. Sort of gives you an image, doesn't it? Luv Dawg. Anyway, the mother laid down the law that Candace wasn't allowed to so much as speak to this guy, who really was a dangerous thug. But Candace had a thing for bad boys. Probably couldn't resist the skull tattoo on his groin. So she and Luv Dawg were getting it on and apparently he didn't care for condoms."

Cassidy leaned her back against the counter in front of the sink. "She got pregnant but didn't want her mother to know who she was doing it with. So she said Jordan forced himself on her." Cassidy stared into space for a moment. "Were the cops able to prove that the girlfriend's story was true?"

"They proved paternity with DNA but couldn't prove the punk killed her. Which was a shame, since he was known for torturing animals and bullying anybody smaller than him."

"Why didn't the cops tell Maxie that Jordan didn't do it?"

"They tried to, but she got hysterical on them. Kept insisting her sweet little girl wouldn't lie to her. Or have anything to do with Luv Dawg."

Cassidy shook her head. "Denial. Maybe the best Maxie could do. The truth might have destroyed her."

"Personally, I think everybody needs a little denial. Most of us couldn't get through the day without it." He reached into the fridge and pulled out a bottle of Sam Adams.

"My husband at his cynical best." She dug an opener out of a drawer and tossed it to him.

"Actually, I can do cynical a lot better than that." He took a swig of beer.

Cassidy held her hands in front of her chest, rubbing one inside the other. "At the beginning of all this, I was in denial about a lot of things. The biggest one was, I couldn't accept that my instincts about Jordan might've been wrong. I couldn't stand to think I'd made a bad call when I decided he wasn't dangerous."

"But you didn't. Your instincts were right."

"In this instance they were. But I could easily have been wrong. My denial—or maybe hubris—is in thinking my gut's always right. The fact is, nobody's always right. I thought Jill was a nice person and look how wrong I was about her."

Stepping closer, Zach rested his arms on her shoulders. "You're right a lot more often than you're wrong.   That ought to be good enough for anybody."

Breinigsville, PA USA
04 February 2011
254852BV00001B/1/P